IMO

OLYMPIAD WORKBOOK

7

INTERNATIONAL MATHEMATICS OLYMPIAD

AF390169

01 Learning Objectives

02 Multiple Choice Questions

03 HOTS (Achievers Section)

04 Model Test Paper

05 Answer Keys and Solutions

06 OMR Answer Sheet

V&S PUBLISHERS

Published by:

V&S PUBLISHERS

F-2/16, Ansari road, Daryaganj, New Delhi-110002
☎ 23240026, 23240027 • *Fax:* 011-23240028
✉ info@vspublishers.com • ⊕ www.vspublishers.com

Online Brandstore: amazon.in/vspublishers

Regional Office : Hyderabad
5-1-707/1, Brij Bhawan (Beside Central Bank of India Lane)
Bank Street, Koti, Hyderabad - 500 095
☎ 040-24737290
✉ vspublishershyd@gmail.com

Follow us on:   

BUY OUR BOOKS FROM: AMAZON FLIPKART

DISCLAIMER

PUBLISHER'S NOTE

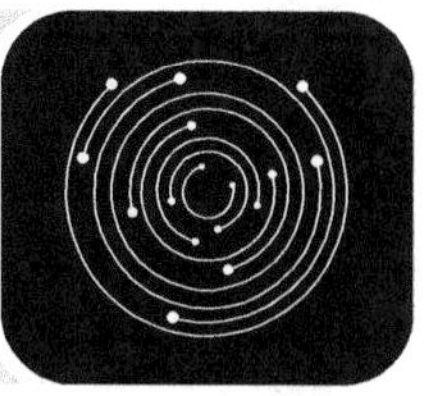

V&S Publishers has carved a significant niche in the publishing industry over the last decade, having successfully published more than 1000 titles across 9 languages spanning over 50 subject categories. Being known for the quality of content, we have built a reputation of excellence and reliability. We have consistently delivered **"Value & Substance"** to our readers, through a wide range of titles across a variety of genres covering school books, fiction and non-fiction that caters to different people from every section of the society.

The **Olympiad Guidebooks for classes 1-10** across all subjects, launched almost a decade ago, under the **GEN X Imprint**, became a go-to-source for the school students in no time, owing to their invaluable and substantive content written in a guidebook pattern,.

Having successfully sold a million copies of the same and in response to demand by both students as well as shopkeepers nationwide; we now present before you our newly launched **Olympiad Workbook Series**, designed for **classes 1-10 across 4 subjects**.

The workbooks are meticulously curated by a team of experienced educators, researchers and subject matter experts, edited by professionals and peer reviewed by teachers. The team has poured its efforts and expertise into creating a crisp and concise workbook which will help and guide the students to the path of success in Olympiad exams. The **MCQs** identified will not only help in scoring top marks in Olympiads but also inculcate a sense of deeper understanding of the subject, by way of solving **HOTS** and referring to complete solutions at the end of the book.

Here we present our new release– **OLYMPIAD WORKBOOK (IMO) CLASS–7** having following features:

- ☞ Based on the latest syllabi
- ☞ MCQs with comprehensive coverage of topics
- ☞ HOTS Questions liberally included
- ☞ A dedicated chapter on logical reasoning
- ☞ Model test paper for thorough practice
- ☞ Sample OMR sheet for real time simulation

We have made sure through our best efforts, that this workbook strictly follows the latest syllabi and patterns of the Olympiad Examination.

As **V&S Publishers** continuously strive to enhance the readability and maintain the credibility of our academic publications, we seek the support of our valuable readers in influencing and enriching the lives of future generations of students.

P.S. While every care has been taken to ensure the correctness of the content, if you come across any error, howsoever minor, do not hesitate to discuss with teachers while pointing that out to us in no uncertain terms.

We wish you all the best for your exams!

DISTINCTIVE FEATURES

01 — Learning Objectives

They list the whole chapter as subtopics, helping the teachers to guide children in a step-by-step manner.

02 — Multiple Choice Questions

MCQs act as an excellent learning aid, helping you to understand and work on your mistakes.

03 — HOTS (Achievers Section)

The High Order Thinking Questions aim to help the student to solve Application-based questions and gain practical understanding of the subject.

04 — Model Test Paper

Model test paper are provided at the end of each book, which help the student to test the knowledge which they have gained after thorough reading of all chapters.

05 — Answer Key

Detailed Answer Key along with explanations aid the pupil to indentify, understand the mistakes they make during the course of Olympiad preparation.

CONTENTS

INTEGERS

1

LEARNING OBJECTIVES

➤ Types of numbers
➤ Operation on integers
➤ Properties of Integers Numbers

MULTIPLE CHOICE QUESTIONS

1. If p and q are two integers such that p is the successor of q, then the value of q − p − 4 is
   (A) −5
   (B) −4
   (C) −3
   (D) −2

2. The value of the expression $63 - 98 - (-58) + 115 + (-172) + 78 + (-62) + 131$ is:
   (A) 341
   (B) 113
   (C) 279
   (D) −3

3. A shopkeeper earns a profit of ₹1 by selling one copy and incure a loss of 40 paise per pen while selling pens of his old stock. In a particular month he incurs a loss of ₹5. In this period he sold 45 copies. How many pens did he sell in this period?
   (A) 175
   (B) 150
   (C) 125
   (D) 100

4. If p and q are two integers such that p > q, then (−p) __________ (−q).
   (A) >
   (B) <
   (C) =
   (D) None of these

5. The temperature of a place is 8°C. Next day the temperature falls by 11°C. What was the temperature of the place on the second day?
   (A) 3ºC
   (B) 19ºC
   (C) −3ºC
   (D) −19ºC

6. A cement company earns a profit of ₹ 8 per bag of white cement sold and a loss of ₹ 5 per bag of grey cement sold. The company sells 3000 bags of white cement and 5000 bags of grey cement in a month. What is its profit or loss?
   (A) ₹ 1000 Loss
   (B) ₹ 1200 Loss
   (C) ₹ 1000 Profit
   (D) ₹ 1200 Profit

7. Sum of two negative numbers is always __________.
   (A) Positive
   (B) Negative
   (C) 0
   (D) 1

8. The temperature at 12 noon was 10°C. It decreased at the rate of 2°C per hour until midnight. At what time would the temperature be 8°C below zero?
   (A) 6 P.M.
   (B) 7 P.M.
   (C) 8 P.M.
   (D) 9 P.M.

9. The price of a stock decreases ₹35 per day for seven consecutive days. What will be the price of the stock after a week if its current price is ₹500?
   (A) ₹ 235
   (B) ₹ 265
   (C) ₹ 245
   (D) ₹ 255

10. A group of hikers started descending from a mountain peak at a rate of 500 metres per hour. At what height are the hikers standing on the mountain after 7 hours if the total height of the mountain is 6048 metres?

(A) 2548 metres   (B) 2458 metres

(C) 3548 metres   (D) 3500 metres

11. An elevator descends into a mine shaft at the rate of 4 m/min. If the descent starts from 14m above the ground level, how long will it take to reach 250 m underground?

(A) 64 min   (B) 65 min

(C) 66 min   (D) 67 min

12. $(888 - 777 + 555) = 111 \times$ ___________.

(A) 5   (B) 6

(C) 7   (D) 8

13. What is simplified value of

$[14 - \{12 - \{9 - (7 - 6 - 2)\}\}]$?

(A) 4   (B) 6

(C) 8   (D) 12

14. Kiran got on an elevator and rode up 13 floors. Next, she rode down 5 floors. After that she went up 6 floors. Finally, she went down 8 floors. When she got off the elevator, she was on 7th floor. From which floor did she start her ride?

(A) 6th   (B) 1st

(C) 5th   (D) 2nd

15. Which of the following will always be an odd integer for all values of p?

(A) 2011p   (B) p^3

(C) $p^2 + 2011$ (D) $2p^2 + 2011$

16. When the integers 9, −7, −2, −4, 1, −1 and 3 are arranged in ascending order, then which of the following integer will come in the middle?

(A) −1   (B) 1

(C) 3   (D) −2

17. Observe the number line and state which of the following statement is not true?

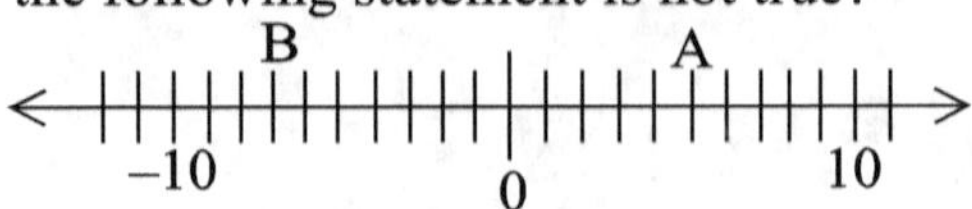

(A) B is greater than −4.

(B) A is smaller than 7

(C) B is smaller than −5.

(D) A is greater than 2.

18. Which of the following letter represents the integer 0?

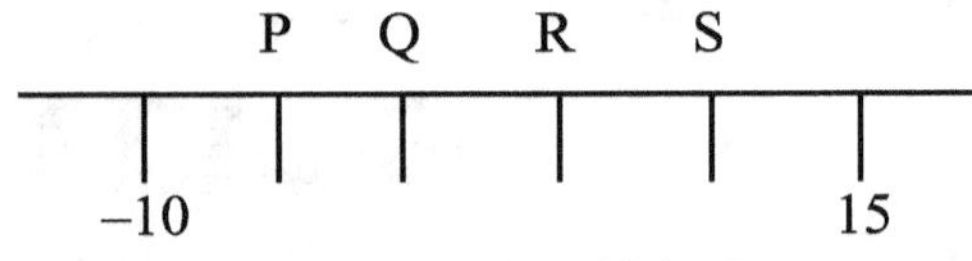

(A) p   (B) Q

(C) R   (D) S

19. If @, #, $ and & represent some integers on the number line, then the ascending order of the integers is:

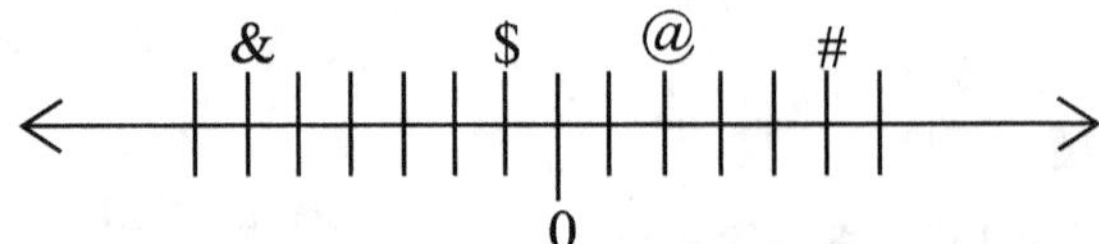

(A) &$@#   (B) @$#&

(C) $#&@   (D) #@$&

20. Which of the following shows the maximum rise in temperature?

(A) 23° to 32°

(B) −10° to +1°

(C) −18° to −11°

(D) −5° to 5°

21. N is the number 1111...ll formed by writing 1004 ones in a row. What is the sum of the digits of the product 1004 x N?
    (A) 10,040
    (B) 11,004
    (C) 4,016
    (D) 5,020

22. Sunita lights a candle every fifteen minutes. Each candle burns for 45 minutes and then goes out. How many candles are alight 75 minutes after Sunita lit the first candle?
    (A) 4
    (B) 5
    (C) 6
    (D) 7

23. An ion is a charged particle whose charge is the sum of the charge on electrons (−1) and the charge on protons (+1). What is the charge on the electrons of an oxide ion having a charge of (−2) and whose proton charge is 8?
    (A) 6
    (B) 8
    (C) −10
    (D) −9

24. A diver descends 20 feet in the water from a boat at the surface of a lake. He then rose 12 feet and descends another 18 feet. At this point what is his depth in water?
    (A) 10 feet
    (B) 26 feet
    (C) 12 feet
    (D) 18 feet

25. In a test (+5) marks are given for every correct answer and (−2) marks are given for every incorrect answer. Sapna answered all the questions and scored 30 marks and got 10 correct answers. Karan also answered all the questions and scored (−12) marks though he got 4 correct answers. How many incorrect answers had they attempted altogether?
    (A) 10
    (B) 16
    (C) 18
    (D) 26

FRACTIONS AND DECIMALS

LEARNING OBJECTIVES

➤ Fractions and its operations
➤ Decimals and its operations

MULTIPLE CHOICE QUESTIONS

1. Which letter comes $\frac{2}{5}$ of the way between A and J?
   (A) D
   (B) E
   (C) F
   (D) G

2. If $\frac{2}{3}$ of a number is 10, then what is 1.75 times of that number?
   (A) 26.24
   (B) 24.26
   (C) 25.26
   (D) 26.25

3. In a class of 40 students, $\frac{1}{5}$ of the total number of students like to eat rice only, $\frac{2}{5}$ of the total number of students like to eat chapati only and the remaining students like to eat both. What fraction of the total number of students like to eat both?
   (A) $\frac{1}{5}$
   (B) $\frac{4}{5}$
   (C) $\frac{2}{5}$
   (D) $\frac{3}{5}$

4. Reetu read $\frac{1}{5}$ th pages of a book. If she reads further 40 pages, she would have read $\frac{7}{10}$ th pages of the book. How many pages are left to be read?
   (A) 23
   (B) 24
   (C) 25
   (D) 26

5. The quotient of $7\frac{1}{6} \div 3\frac{2}{3}$ is:
   (A) Equal to 1.5
   (B) Less than 1.5
   (C) Greater than 1.5
   (D) None of these

6. Simplify: $\dfrac{2\frac{1}{2}+\frac{1}{5}}{2\frac{1}{2}\div\frac{1}{5}}$
   (A) $\frac{18}{125}$
   (B) $\frac{12}{125}$
   (C) $\frac{36}{125}$
   (D) $\frac{27}{125}$

7. The normal body temperature is 98.6° F. When Savitri was ill, her temperature rose to 103.1° F. How many degrees above normal was that?
   (A) 4.5°F
   (B) 2.5°F
   (C) 1.5°F
   (D) 3.5°F

8. What number divided by 520 gives the same quotient as 85 divided by 0.625?
   (A) 72000
   (B) 77200
   (C) 70720
   (D) 72700

9. How much cloth will be used in making 6 shirts, if each shirt requires $2\frac{1}{4}$ m of cloth, allowing $\frac{1}{8}$ m for waste in cutting and finishing each shirt?
   (A) $12\frac{1}{4}$ m
   (B) $12\frac{3}{4}$ m

(C) $14\frac{3}{4}$ m (D) $14\frac{1}{4}$ m

10. A picture hall has seats for 820 people. At a recent film show, one usher guessed it was $\frac{3}{4}$ full, another that it was $\frac{2}{3}$ full. The ticket office reported 648 sales. Which usher (first or second) made the better guess?
(A) First usher (B) Second usher
(C) Both ushers (D) None of them

11. How many pieces of plywood each 0.35 cm thick are required to make a pile 1.89 m high?
(A) 520 (B) 530
(C) 540 (D) 560

12. A car covers a distance of 31.8 km in 2.4 litres of petrol. How much distance will it cover in 5 litres of petrol?
(A) 64.25 km
(B) 66.25 km
(C) 66.75 km
(D) None of these

13. Each side of a polygon is 3.9 cm and its perimeter is 31.2 cm. How many sides does the polygon have?
(A) 6 (B) 7
(C) 8 (D) 9

14. $0.4 \div 0.4 \div 0.4 = ?$

(A) 0.25 (B) 0.025
(C) 2.5 (D) None of these

15. Mukesh bought 17.5 litres of mustard oil for ₹1550.50. What is the cost per litre?
(A) ₹86.7 (B) ₹87.6
(C) ₹88.6 (D) ₹89.6

16. A bus can cover 31.25 km in half an hour. How much distance can it cover in 16 hours ?
(A) 750 km (B) 850 km
(C) 950 km (D) 1000 km

17. $(0.25)^2 - (0.19)^2 = ?$
(A) 0.0264 (B) 0.264
(C) 2.64 (D) 0.204

18. What is the product of $11.1 \times 1.1 \times 0.11$?
(A) 13.401 (B) 1.3031
(C) 13.431 (D) 1.3431

19. Mohan purchased a notebook for ₹27.75, a pencil for ₹4.25 and a pen for ₹26.45. He gives a 100 rupee note to the shopkeeper. What amount did he get back?
(A) ₹41.55 (B) ₹42.55
(C) ₹43.55 (D) None of these

20. Find the simplified value of
$79.1 - 27.73 + 18.07 - 46.37$
(A) 23.07 (B) 24.07
(C) 23.87 (D) 23.67

HOTS (ACHIEVERS SECTION)

21. Look at the alphabets given.

P R A S A D

What fraction of alphabets are made of semicircles and straight lines?
(A) 12 (B) 25
(C) 56 (D) 45

22. Which of the following is an improper fraction?

(A) 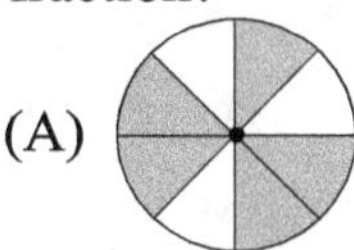

(B) 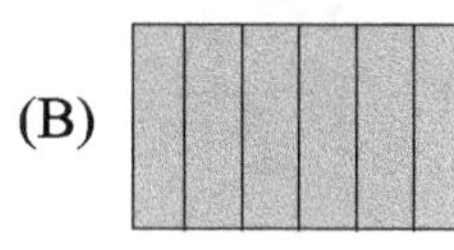

(C) 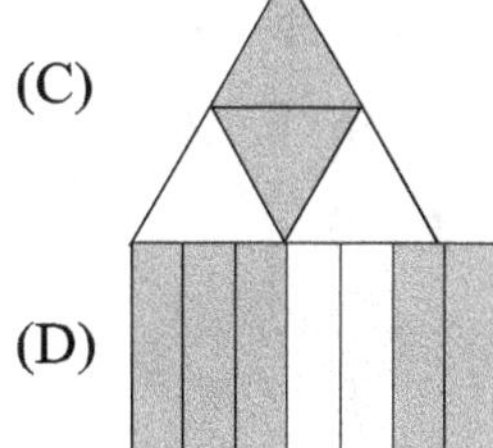

(D)

23. What does the shaded part of the following strip represent?

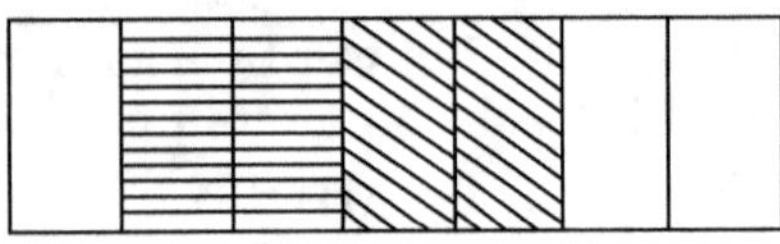

(A) $27 - 17 + 27 = 37$
(B) $27 + 17 - 27 = 17$
(C) $27 + 17 = 37$
(D) $17 + 27 + 27 = 57$

24. What is the decimal fraction shown by the shaded part of the figure given?

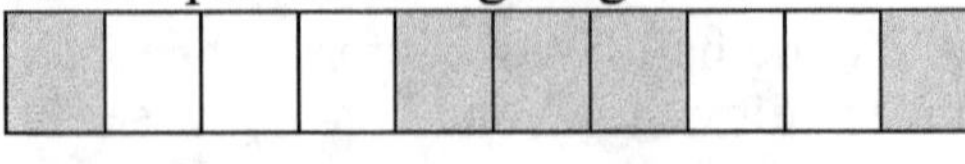

(A) 2.5   (B) 0.5
(C) 0.6   (D) 0.4

25. Find $78.5 \div 0.5$?

(A) 153   (B) 159
(C) 158   (D) 157

DATA HANDLING

3

➤ Basics of Data
➤ Frequency

MULTIPLE CHOICE QUESTIONS

1. What is the median of first 15 odd numbers?
   (A) 15   (B) 17
   (C) 19   (D) 21

2. What is the median of first 50 whole numbers?
   (A) 25.5
   (B) 24.5
   (C) 26.5
   (D) None of these

3. What is the median of 21, 15, 8, 28, 19, 23, 40, 7, 16, 9, 22 ?
   (A) 16   (B) 19
   (C) 21   (D) 22

4. What is the mode of the following data 22, 28, 47, 43, 28, 27, 36, 43, 45, 42, 43, 46, ?
   (A) 22   (B) 28
   (C) 47   (D) None of these

5. If the mean of a given data is 51kg and its median is 50 kg, what is the mode of that data?
   (A) 52 kg   (B) 51 kg
   (C) 53 kg   (D) 54 kg

6. If the mode of the given data is 22.16, its median is 22. What is its mean?
   (A) 20.92   (B) 21.92
   (C) 22.92   (D) 23.92

7. What is the mean of first 12 multiples of 7?
   (A) 45   (B) 46
   (C) 45.5   (D) 46.5

8. What is the median of the given data?

Marks obtained (x_i)	17	20	25	22	15	30
Number of students (f_i)	5	9	6	4	3	10

   (A) 17   (B) 20
   (C) 22   (D) None of these

9. What is the mean of the given data?

Weight in kg	60	63	65	72	75	77
No. of labours	4	5	4	2	6	3

   (A) 67.33   (B) 64.33
   (C) 68.33   (D) None of these

10. What is the median of first 9 multiples of 12?
    (A) 36   (B) 48
    (C) 60   (D) 72

11. What is the mode of the given data 16, 20, 8, 17, 27, 34, 28, 32, 27, 15, 27, 54, 42.
    (A) 8   (B) 27
    (C) 54   (D) None of these

12. If the mean of the given data 16, 24, x, 34, 35, 25, 37, 42, 47, is 32. What is the value of x?
(A) 26   (B) 27
(C) 28   (D) 29

13. The heights of nine players of a team are 165cm, 168cm, 170cm, 174cm, 182cm, 160cm, 171cm, 173cm, 164cm. Find the median.
(A) 168 cm   (B) 170 cm
(C) 171 cm   (D) None of these

14. What is the mean of the following data?

Marks obtained	45	27	20	56	82	75	17
No. of students	5	3	8	7	2	4	12

(A) 34.22   (B) 36.22
(C) 37.22   (D) None of these

15. What is the median of the following data?

Marks obtained	72	47	62	57	42	52	67
No. of students	9	8	11	8	3	6	5

(A) 56.5   (B) 57.5
(C) 58.5   (D) 59.5

16. The ages in years of 15 teachers of a school are 41, 32, 51, 43, 24, 38, 49, 56, 42, 28, 37, 48, 45, 47, 50. What is the range of ages of teachers?
(A) 32 years   (B) 30 years
(C) 28 years   (D) None of these

17. A batsman scored the following number of runs in 8 innings. What is the arithmetic mean? 59, 36, 57, 35, 60, 55, 46, 50.
(A) 49.25   (B) 49.35
(C) 49.65   (D) 49.75

18. Following are the margins of victory in the football matches of a league.

1, 3, 2, 5, 1, 4, 6, 2, 5, 2, 2, 2, 4, 1, 2, 3, 1, 1, 2, 3, 2, 6, 4, 3, 2, 1, 1, 4, 2, 1, 5, 3, 3, 2, 3, 2, 4, 2, 1, 2.

What is the mode of this data?
(A) 1   (B) 2
(C) 3   (D) 4

19. The scores in physics test (out of 100) of 15 students is as follows: 19, 42, 68, 27, 36, 48, 78, 38, 12, 17, 61, 65, 47, 84, 39. What is the median of this data?
(A) 39   (B) 42
(C) 47   (D) 48

20. What is the mode of this following data: 12, 14, 12, 16, 15, 13, 14, 18, 19, 12, 14, 15, 16, 15, 16, 16, 15. 17, 13, 16, 16, 15, 15, 13, 15, 17, 15, 14, 15, 13, 15, 14.
(A) 13   (B) 14
(C) 15   (D) 16

HOTS (ACHIEVERS SECTION)

21. In a Mathematics test following marks were obtained by 40 students of class VI. Arrange these marks in a table using, tally marks.

8	1	3	7	6	5	5	4	4	2
4	9	5	3	7	1	6	5	2	7
7	3	8	4	2	6	9	5	8	6
7	4	5	6	9	6	4	4	6	6

How many students obtained marks equal to or more than 7?
(A) 10   (B) 24
(C) 25   (D) 3

22. In a Mathematics test following marks were obtained by 40 students of class VI. Arrange these marks in a table using, tally marks.

8	1	3	7	6	5	5	4	4	2
4	9	5	3	7	1	6	5	2	7
7	3	8	4	2	6	9	5	8	6
7	4	5	6	9	6	4	4	6	6

How many students obtained marks below 4?
(A) 10   (B) 24
(C) 11   (D) 14

23. If the heights of 5 persons are 140 cm, 150 cm, 152 cm, 158 cm and 161 cm respectively, the mean height will be:

(A) 152.2 cm   (B) 132.5 cm

(C) 130.4 cm   (D) 125.2 cm

24. The mean of first 10 even natural numbers:

(A) 13   (B) 10

(C) 11   (D) 12

25. The following data gives the amount of manure (in thousand tonnes) manufactured by a company during some years:

Year	1992	1993	1994	1995	1996	1997
Manure (in thousand tonnes)	15	35	45	30	40	20

The consecutive years during which there was maximum decrease in manure production are:

(A) 1994 and 1995   (B) 1992 and 1993

(C) 1996 and 1997   (D) 1995 and 1996

SIMPLE EQUATIONS

4

➤ Linear equation of one variable and its solution

MULTIPLE CHOICE QUESTIONS

1. Mr. Sharma left one-third of his property to his daughter, one-fourth to his son and the remainder to his wife. If his wife's share is ₹18000 what was the worth of Mr. Sharma's total property?
   (A) ₹41200 (B) ₹42200
   (C) ₹43200 (D) ₹44200

2. In an examination, a student requires 40% of the total marks to pass. If Manoj gets 185 marks and fails by 15 marks what is the total marks?
   (A) 400 (B) 500
   (C) 550 (D) 600

3. 50 kg of an alloy of nickel and iron contains 60% nickel. How much nickel must be melted into it to make the alloy contain 75% of nickel?
   (A) 20 kg (B) 30 kg
   (C) 35 kg (D) 40 kg

4. The sum of digits of a two digit number is 9. If 27 is added to the number its digits get interchanged. What is the number?
   (A) 36 (B) 63
   (C) 46 (D) 64

5. Solve for x, $x - \left(2x - \dfrac{3x - 4}{7}\right) = \dfrac{4x - 27}{3} - 3$.
   (A) 40 (B) 60
   (C) 50 (D) 45

6. A bookseller earned a profit of 5% by selling a book for ₹714. What is the cost price of the book?
   (A) ₹620 (B) ₹640
   (C) ₹660 (D) ₹680

7. The length of a rectangle is three times of its breadth. Its perimeter is 128m, what is its length?
   (A) 24 m
   (B) 36 m
   (C) 48 m
   (D) None of these

8. Ramesh travelled $\dfrac{3}{5}$ of his journey by rail, $\dfrac{1}{4}$ by a car, $\dfrac{1}{8}$ by a bus and the remaining 4 km on foot. What is the length of total journey?
   (A) 120 km
   (B) 140 km
   (C) 160 km
   (D) 180 km

9. A number consists of two-digits whose sum is 8. If 18 is added to the number its digits are reversed. What is that number?
   (A) 35 (B) 36
   (C) 53 (D) 63

10. A number is as much greater than 21 as it is less than 71. What is that number?

(A) 36

(B) 46

(C) 48

(D) 56

11. Two supplementary angles differ by 20°. What is the measure of smaller angle?

(A) 30   (B) 40

(C) 80   (D) 100

12. A number when multiplied by 5 is increased by 80. What is that number?

(A) 15   (B) 16

(C) 18   (D) 20

13. The sum of three consecutive odd numbers is 99. What is the difference of smallest and largest odd number?

(A) 1   (B) 2

(C) 3   (D) 4

14. The ages of Simran and Ranjna are in the ratio 5:3. After 6 years their ages will be in the ratio 7:5. What is the present age of Ranjna?

(A) 9 years   (B) 12 years

(C) 14 years   (D) 15 years

15. Thrice a number when increased by 6 gives 84. What is that number?

(A) 26   (B) 28

(C) 32   (D) 34

16. The sum of two consecutive even number is 96. What is the smaller number?

(A) 42   (B) 44

(C) 46   (D) 48

17. On adding nine to the twice of a whole number gives 61. What is $\dfrac{5}{13}$ of that whole number?

(A) 5   (B) 10

(C) 15   (D) 20

18. After 12 years Manish will be three times as old as he was 4 years ago. What is his present age?

(A) 12 years

(B) 14 years

(C) 16 years

(D) 18 years

19. Niraj is 19 years younger than his cousin after 5 years their age will be in the ratio 2:3. What is the present age of Niraj?

(A) 31 years   (B) 33 years

(C) 35 years   (D) 36 years

20. What is the value of p in the given equation $8(2p - 5) - 6(3p - 7) = 1$?

(A) 1   (B) $\dfrac{1}{2}$

(C) $\dfrac{1}{3}$ (D) $\dfrac{1}{4}$

HOTS (ACHIEVERS SECTION)

21. Solving $2(5x - 3) - 3(2x - 1) = 9$ will give value of x as:

(A) 3   (B) 5

(C) 87   (D) 9

22. Solving $\left(\dfrac{x}{2}\right) + \left(\dfrac{3}{2}\right) = \left(\dfrac{2x}{5}\right) - 1$ will give value of x as:

(A) –25   (B) –24

(C) –45   (D) –5

23. Solving $3x - 2(2x - 5) = 2(x + 3) - 8$ will give value of x as:

(A) 4   (B) 5

(C) 8   (D) 6

24. Solving $\left(\dfrac{6x-2}{9}\right)+\left(\dfrac{3x+5}{18}\right)=\left(\dfrac{1}{3}\right)$ will give value of x as:

(A) $\dfrac{4}{3}$ (B) $\dfrac{2}{3}$

(C) $\dfrac{1}{3}$ (D) $\dfrac{10}{3}$

25. Solving $m-\dfrac{(m-1)}{2}=1-\dfrac{(m-2)}{3}$ will give value of m as:

(A) $\dfrac{9}{5}$ (B) $\dfrac{2}{5}$

(C) $\dfrac{1}{5}$ (D) $\dfrac{7}{5}$

⏰ ⏰ ⏰

—Darken Your Choice with HB Pencil—

1.	Ⓐ Ⓑ Ⓒ Ⓓ	6.	Ⓐ Ⓑ Ⓒ Ⓓ	11.	Ⓐ Ⓑ Ⓒ Ⓓ	16	Ⓐ Ⓑ Ⓒ Ⓓ	21.	Ⓐ Ⓑ Ⓒ Ⓓ
2.	Ⓐ Ⓑ Ⓒ Ⓓ	7.	Ⓐ Ⓑ Ⓒ Ⓓ	12.	Ⓐ Ⓑ Ⓒ Ⓓ	17.	Ⓐ Ⓑ Ⓒ Ⓓ	22.	Ⓐ Ⓑ Ⓒ Ⓓ
3.	Ⓐ Ⓑ Ⓒ Ⓓ	8.	Ⓐ Ⓑ Ⓒ Ⓓ	13.	Ⓐ Ⓑ Ⓒ Ⓓ	18.	Ⓐ Ⓑ Ⓒ Ⓓ	23.	Ⓐ Ⓑ Ⓒ Ⓓ
4.	Ⓐ Ⓑ Ⓒ Ⓓ	9.	Ⓐ Ⓑ Ⓒ Ⓓ	14.	Ⓐ Ⓑ Ⓒ Ⓓ	19.	Ⓐ Ⓑ Ⓒ Ⓓ	24.	Ⓐ Ⓑ Ⓒ Ⓓ
5.	Ⓐ Ⓑ Ⓒ Ⓓ	10.	Ⓐ Ⓑ Ⓒ Ⓓ	15.	Ⓐ Ⓑ Ⓒ Ⓓ	20.	Ⓐ Ⓑ Ⓒ Ⓓ	25.	Ⓐ Ⓑ Ⓒ Ⓓ

LINES AND ANGLES

5

LEARNING OBJECTIVES

➤ Parallel lines

➤ Different types of angles

MULTIPLE CHOICE QUESTIONS

1. What is the supplement of 64°?
   (A) 106° (B) 126°
   (C) 116° (D) 26°

2. What is the value of x in the given figure?

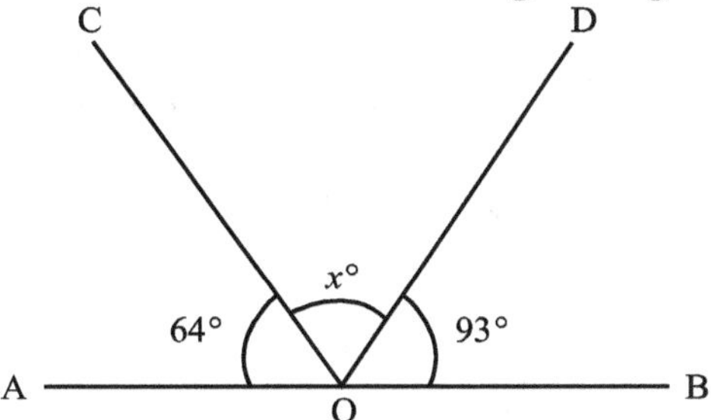

   (A) 23° (B) 33°
   (C) 43° (D) None of these

3. In the given figure two straight lines AB and PQ intersect at a point O. If $\angle AOP = 47°$ what is the measure of $\angle BOQ$?

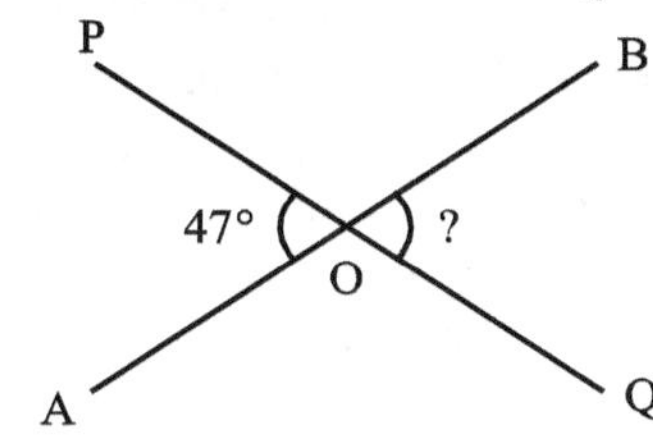

   (A) 47° (B) 133°
   (C) 123° (D) None of these

4. What is the complement of 67°?
   (A) 33° (B) 23°
   (C) 43° (D) None of these

5. In the following figure, if AB ∥ CD, $\angle BAP = 108°$ and $\angle PCD = 120°$, what is the measure of $\angle APC$?

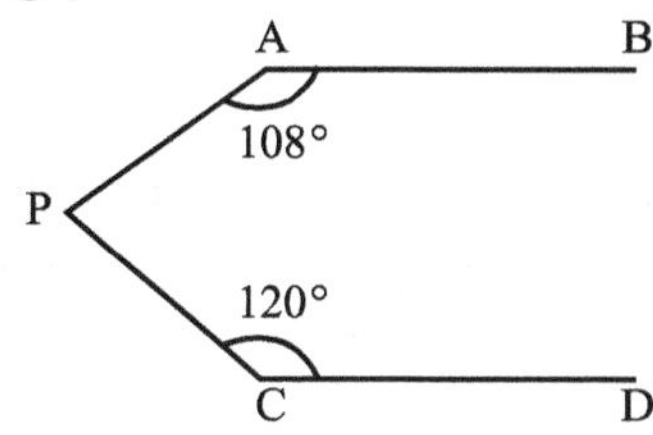

   (A) 72° (B) 92°
   (C) 132° (D) None of these

6. In the given figure MN ∥ PQ $\angle MNE = 120°$, $\angle EPQ = 100°$.

   What is the value of x?

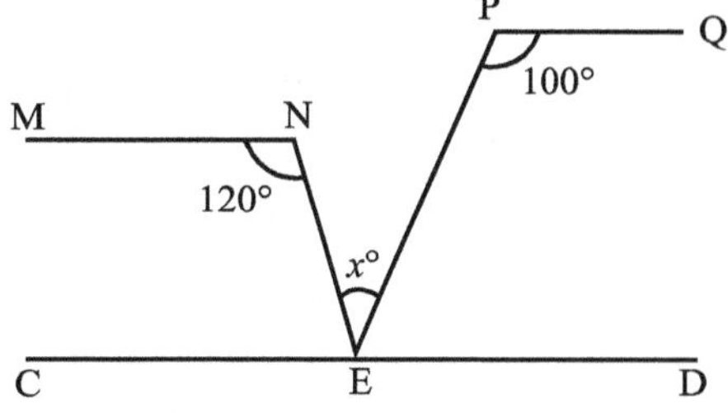

   (A) 20° (B) 30°
   (C) 40° (D) 60°

7. In the given figure AB ∥ CD and EF is transversal. If ∠1 and ∠2 are in the ratio 5:7 what is the measure of ∠8?

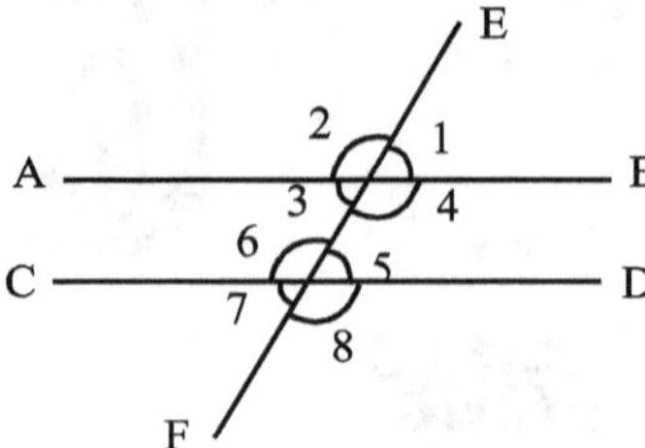

(A) 75°   (B) 105°
(C) 85°   (D) 115°

8. What is the value of x in the following figure?

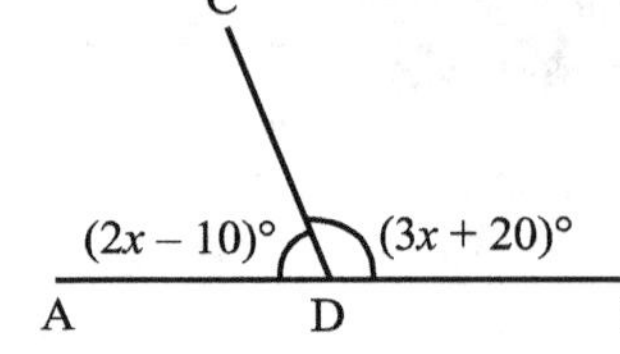

(A) 24°   (B) 34°
(C) 44°   (D) 54°

9. Which of the following angle is its complement?

(A) 30°   (B) 45°
(C) 60°   (D) 90°

10. In the given figure, ABC is a straight line. What is the value of y?

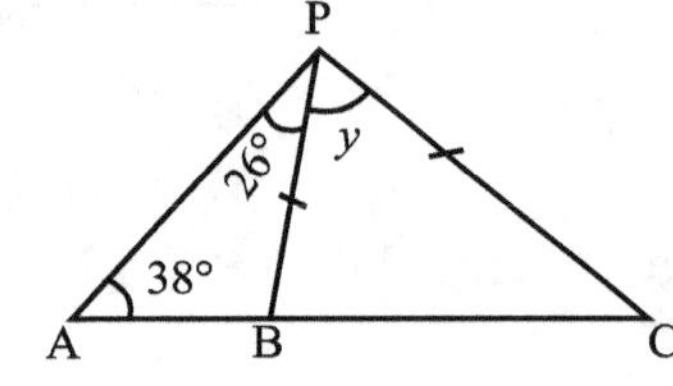

(A) 42°   (B) 52°
(C) 62°   (D) 32°

11. In the given figure, PQR is a straight line. What is the value of x?

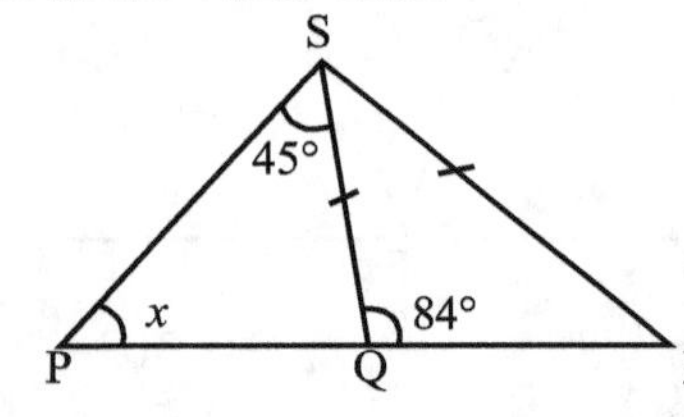

(A) 39°   (B) 49°
(C) 59°   (D) None of these

12. In the given figure, ABC is a straight line what is the value of z?

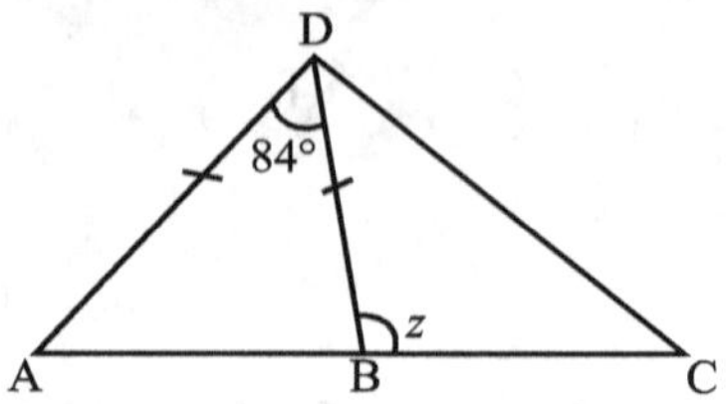

(A) 112°   (B) 92°
(C) 132°   (D) None of these

13. In the given figure, what is the length of BC if AB = AC?

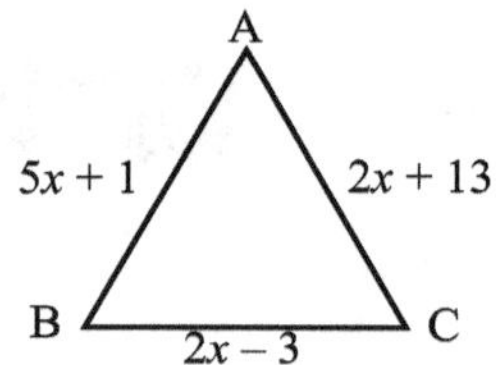

(A) 3   (B) 5
(C) 6   (D) 7

14. In the given figure ΔACD is a right angled triangle. ΔABC is an isosceles triangle with AB = AC. ACQ, EAD, are straight lines. What is the value of x?

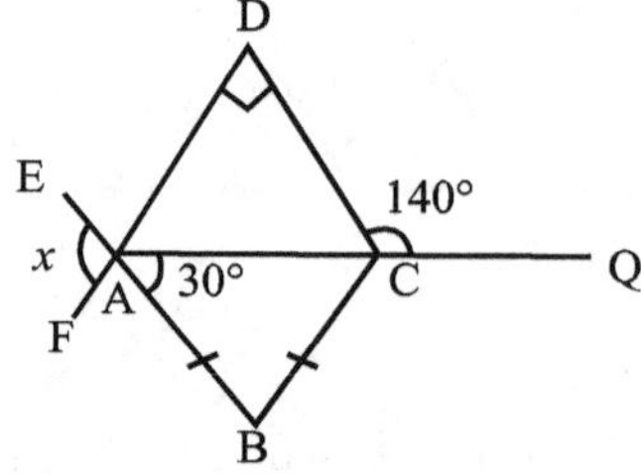

(A) 60°   (B) 70°
(C) 80°   (D) 90°

15. If the sides of a triangle are as given in the figure. The perimeter of triangle is 78 m. What is the measure of the highest side?

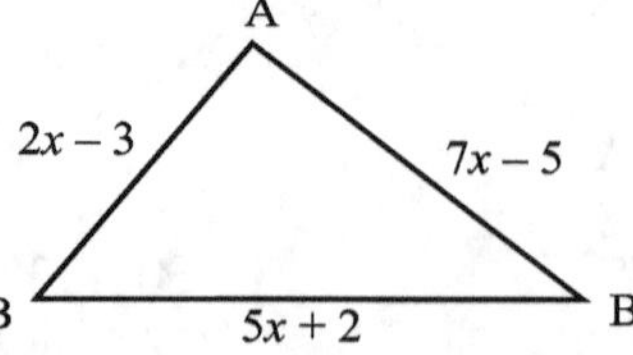

(A) 32 m   (B) 37 m
(C) 35 m   (D) 38 m

16. In the given figure $\triangle ABC$ is an equilateral triangle and $\triangle ACD$ is an isosceles triangle. What is the value of x?

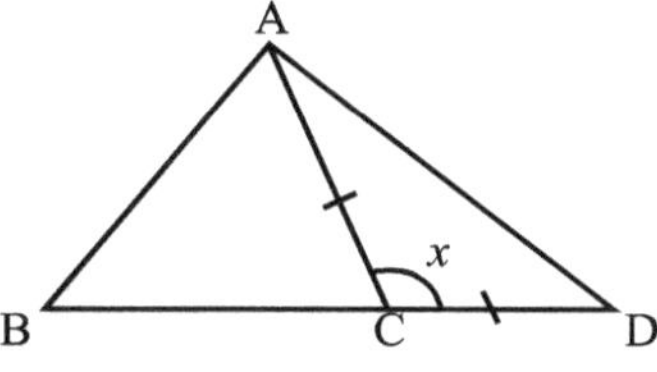

(A) 40° (B) 60°
(C) 120° (D) None of these

17. If l ∥ m, then what is the value of x?

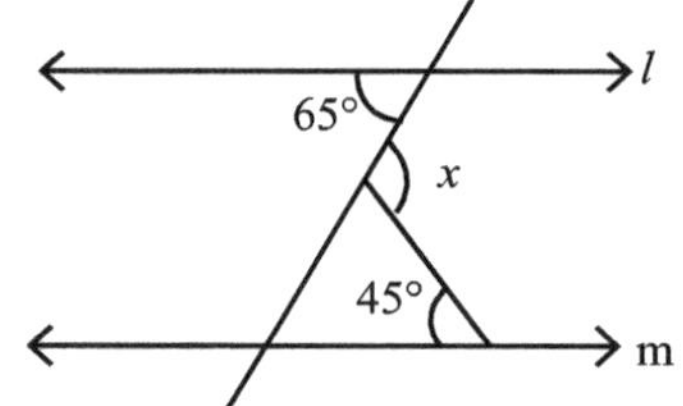

(A) 70° (B) 110°
(C) 65° (D) 25°

18. In the given figure, $\dfrac{y}{x} = 5$ and $\dfrac{z}{x} = 4$

then what is the value of x?

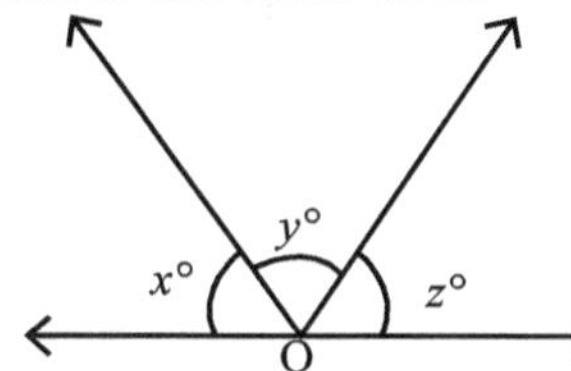

(A) 18° (B) 12°
(C) 28° (D) 15°

19. Find the value of x in figure given below.

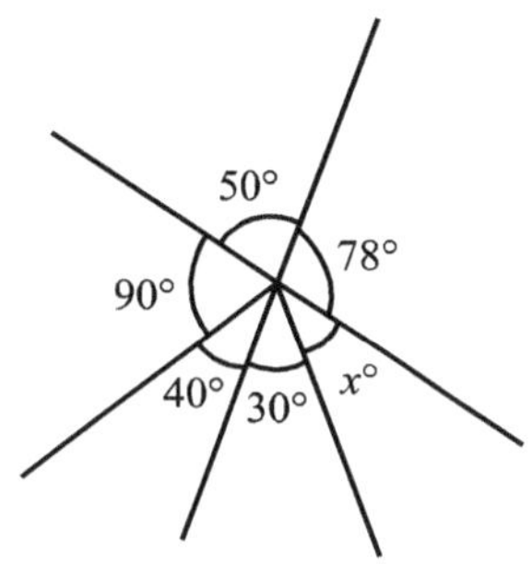

(A) 72°
(B) 82°
(C) 92°
(D) 42°

20. $\angle A = 56°$, CE ∥ BA $\angle ECD = 73°$. What is the value of $\angle ACD$?

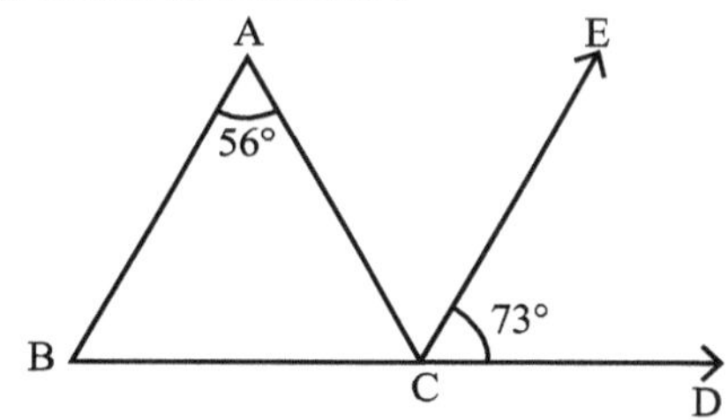

(A) 31°
(B) 41°
(C) 51°
(D) 61°

HOTS (ACHIEVERS SECTION)

21. In Figure below, OA and OB are opposite rays. If $x = 25°$, what is the value of y?

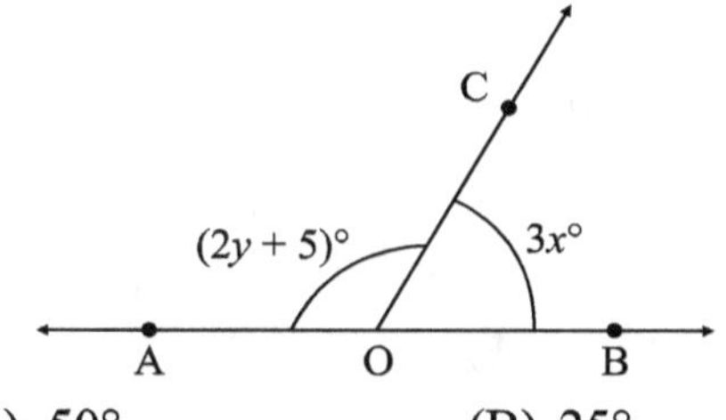

(A) 50° (B) 25°
(C) 55° (D) 70°

22. In Figure below, OA and OB are opposite rays. If $y = 35°$, what is the value of x?

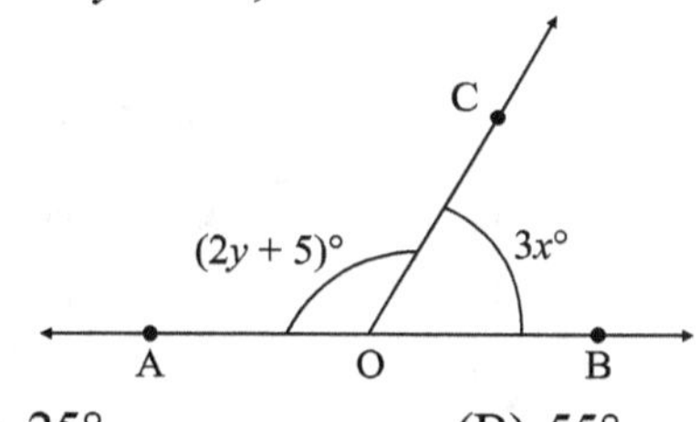

(A) 25° (B) 55°
(C) 35° (D) 45°

23. In Figure below, find ∠*x*. Further find ∠BOC.

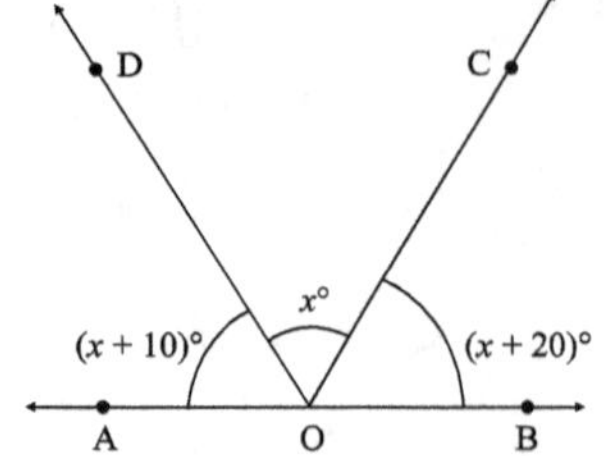

(A) 50° , 70°   (B) 50° , 60°

(C) 50° , 80°   (D) 50° , 40°

24. In Figure below, find ∠*x*. Further find ∠COD.

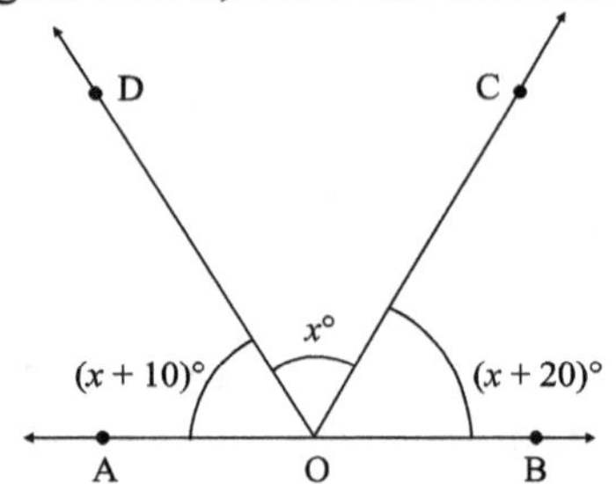

(A) 50° , 30°

(B) 50° , 50°

(C) 50° , 60°

(D) 50° , 70°

25. In Figure below, find ∠*x*. Further find ∠AOD.

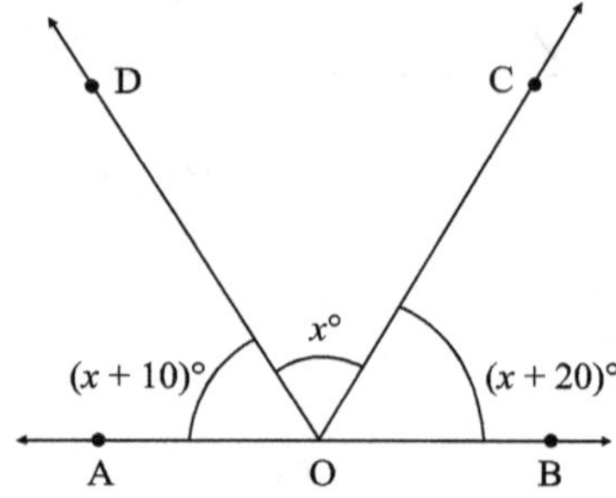

(A) 50°, 50°

(B) 50° , 70°

(C) 50° , 60°

(D) 50° , 80°

Darken Your Choice with HB Pencil

1. Ⓐ Ⓑ Ⓒ Ⓓ	6. Ⓐ Ⓑ Ⓒ Ⓓ	11. Ⓐ Ⓑ Ⓒ Ⓓ	16 Ⓐ Ⓑ Ⓒ Ⓓ	21. Ⓐ Ⓑ Ⓒ Ⓓ
2. Ⓐ Ⓑ Ⓒ Ⓓ	7. Ⓐ Ⓑ Ⓒ Ⓓ	12. Ⓐ Ⓑ Ⓒ Ⓓ	17. Ⓐ Ⓑ Ⓒ Ⓓ	22. Ⓐ Ⓑ Ⓒ Ⓓ
3. Ⓐ Ⓑ Ⓒ Ⓓ	8. Ⓐ Ⓑ Ⓒ Ⓓ	13. Ⓐ Ⓑ Ⓒ Ⓓ	18. Ⓐ Ⓑ Ⓒ Ⓓ	23. Ⓐ Ⓑ Ⓒ Ⓓ
4. Ⓐ Ⓑ Ⓒ Ⓓ	9. Ⓐ Ⓑ Ⓒ Ⓓ	14. Ⓐ Ⓑ Ⓒ Ⓓ	19. Ⓐ Ⓑ Ⓒ Ⓓ	24. Ⓐ Ⓑ Ⓒ Ⓓ
5. Ⓐ Ⓑ Ⓒ Ⓓ	10. Ⓐ Ⓑ Ⓒ Ⓓ	15. Ⓐ Ⓑ Ⓒ Ⓓ	20. Ⓐ Ⓑ Ⓒ Ⓓ	25. Ⓐ Ⓑ Ⓒ Ⓓ

THE TRIANGLES & PROPERTIES

LEARNING OBJECTIVES

➤ Basic of Triangles

➤ Different types of Triangles

MULTIPLE CHOICE QUESTIONS

1. Two angles of a triangle are equal and the third angle measures 70°. Find the measure of each of the unknown angles.
   (A) 50°　　　　　　(B) 55°
   (C) 70°　　　　　　(D) 110°

2. In a $\triangle XYZ$, if $\angle X = 90°$ and $\angle Z = 48°$, find $\angle Y$.
   (A) 42°　　　　　　(B) 45°
   (C) 40°　　　　　　(D) 35°

3. Each of the two equal angles of an isosceles triangle is twice the third angle. Find the angles of the triangle.
   (A) 36°, 72°, 36°
   (B) 45°, 60°, 75°
   (C) 36°, 36°, 72°
   (D) 72°, 72°, 36°

4. What is the measure of each angle of an equilateral triangle?
   (A) 60°　　　　　　(B) 80°
   (C) 40°　　　　　　(D) 70°

5. Find the angles of a triangle which are in the ratio 4 : 3 : 2.
   (A) 15°, 20°, 25°
   (B) 20°, 20°, 40°
   (C) 80°, 60°, 40°
   (D) 40°, 80°, 60°

6. In the given figure, find the values of x and y.

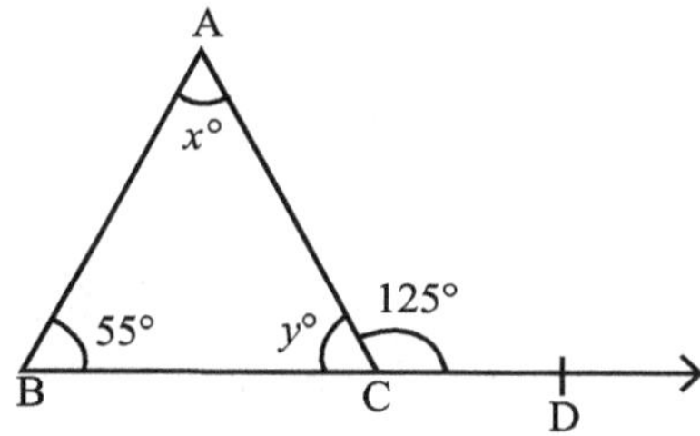

   (A) $x = 55°, y = 70°$
   (B) $x = 55°, y = 55°$
   (C) $x = 50°, y = 70°$
   (D) $x = 70°, y = 55°$

7. In the given figure, find the values of x and y.

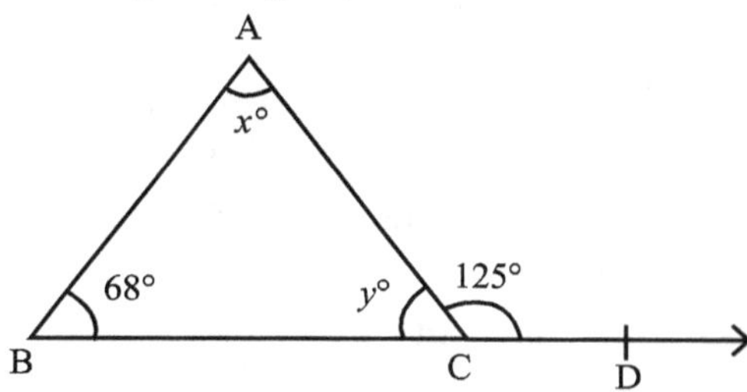

   (A) $y = 62°, x = 50°$
   (B) $x = 62°, y = 50°$
   (C) $x = 52°, y = 40°$
   (D) $x = 50°, y = 60°$

8. In the figure given alongside, $x : y = 2 : 3$ and $\angle ACD = 130°$ find the values of x, y and z.

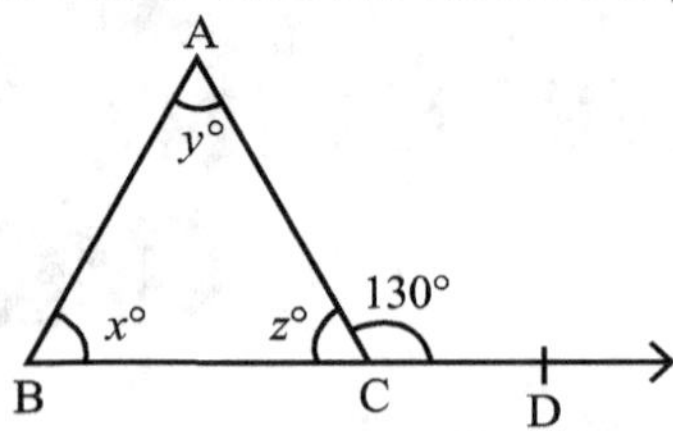

   (A) $x = 26°, y = 52°, z = 26°$
   (B) $x = 50°, y = 80°, z = 50°$
   (C) $x = 52°, y = 78°, z = 50°$
   (D) $x = 50°, y = 78°, z = 52°$

9. A man goes 24m due east and then 10m due north. How far is he away from his initial position?
   (A) 24 m
   (B) 28 m
   (C) 30 m
   (D) 26 m

10. The lengths of the sides of two triangles are given below. Which of them is right – angled?
    (i) $a = 8$ cm, $b = 5$ cm, and $c = 10$ cm
    (ii) $a = 7$ cm, $b = 24$ cm, and $c = 25$ cm
    (A) (i) and (ii) both
    (B) (ii) is but (i) not
    (C) (i) and (ii) both not
    (D) None of these

11. Two poles of height 9 cm and 14m stand upright on a plane ground. If the distance between their feet is 12 m. Find the distance between their tops.
    (A) 12 m
    (B) 13 m
    (C) 5 m
    (D) 15 m

12. Two circles are congruent if they have
    (A) Same length
    (B) Same breadth
    (C) Same radius
    (D) None of these

13. Two lines segments are congruent if they have
    (A) The same length
    (B) Same breadth
    (C) Same radius
    (D) None of these

14. In a $\triangle ABC$ it is given that $\angle B = 37°$ and $\angle C = 29°$. Then $\angle A = ?$

    (A) 57°
    (B) 114°
    (C) 66°
    (D) 86°

15. In a $\triangle ABC$, if $2\angle A = 3$, $\angle B = 6\angle C$ then $\angle B = ?$
    (A) 30°
    (B) 90°
    (C) 60°
    (D) 45°

16. In a $\triangle ABC$, $\angle A - \angle B = 33°$ and $\angle B - \angle C = 18°$, then $\angle B = ?$
    (A) 35°
    (B) 55°
    (C) 45°
    (D) 57°

17. The sum of all angles of a triangle is
    (A) 90°
    (B) 150°
    (C) 100°
    (D) 180°

18. In the given figure, what value of x will make AOB a straight line?

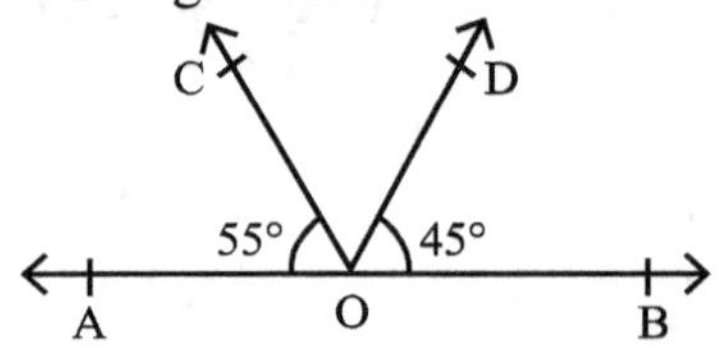

    (A) $x = 50$
    (B) $x = 80$
    (C) $x = 100$
    (D) $x = 60$

19. In the given figure, AOB is a straight line, $\angle AOC = (3x - 8)°$, $\angle COD = 50°$ and $\angle BOD = (x + 10)°$. The value of x is

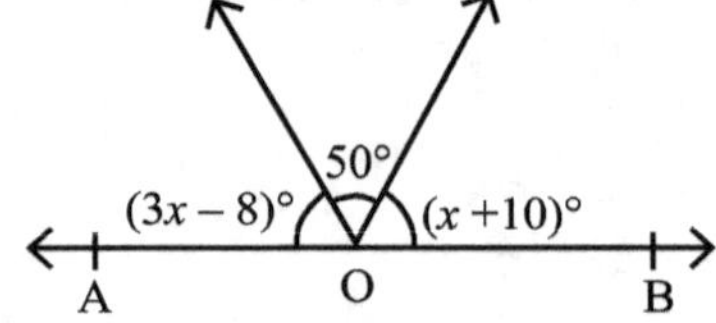

    (A) 42
    (B) 52
    (C) 36
    (D) 32

20. In $\triangle ABC$, $\angle B = 90°$, $AB = 5$cm and $AC = 13$cm then $BC = ?$

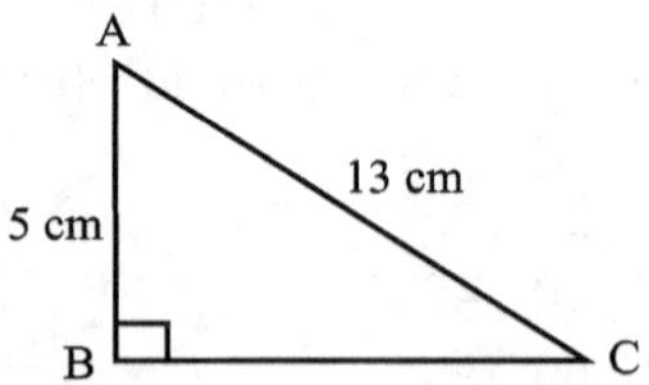

    (A) 18 cm
    (B) 12 cm
    (C) 8 cm
    (D) None of these

21. In the following figure, if $l \parallel m$ value of a will be:

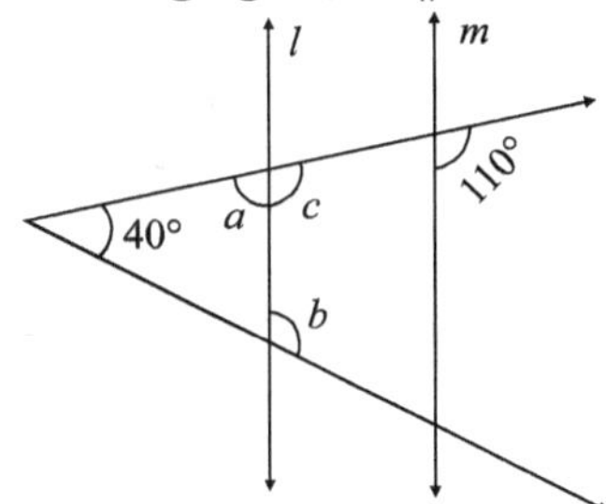

(A) 180°
(B) 110°
(C) 70°
(D) 40°

22. In the following figure, if $l \parallel m$ value of b will be:

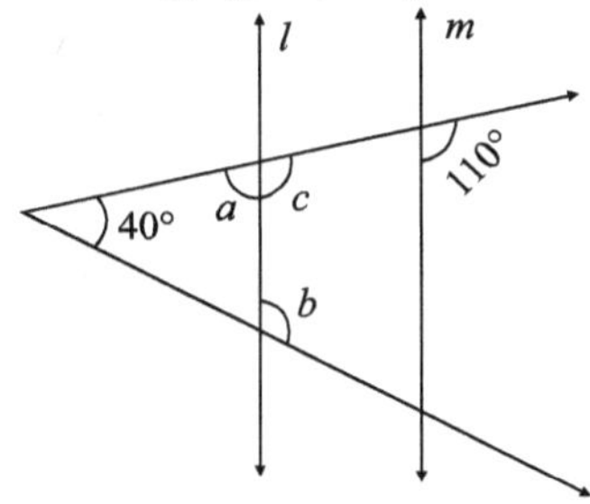

(A) 180°   (B) 110°
(C) 70°   (D) 40°

23. Find the values of a, b and c.

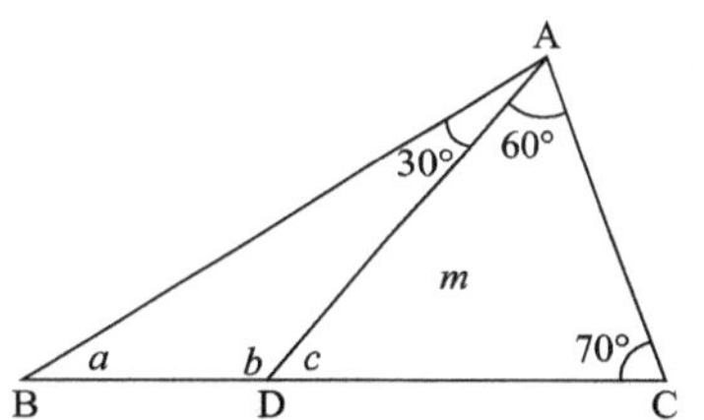

(A) $a = 20°$, $b = 130°$ and $c = 50°$
(B) $a = 50°$, $b = 130°$ and $c = 20°$
(C) $a = 10°$, $b = 130°$ and $c = 20°$
(D) $a = 20°$, $b = 30°$ and $c = 40°$

24. Find the values of a, b and c.

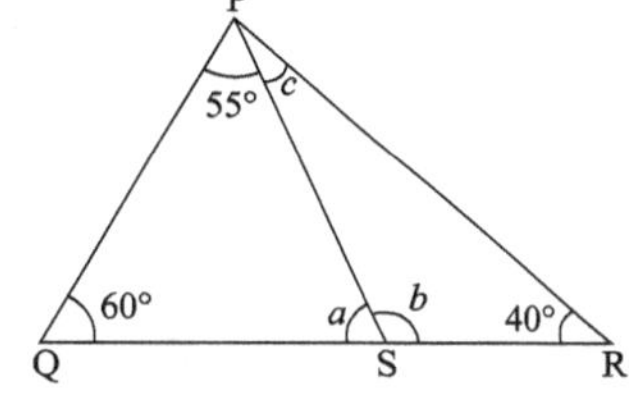

(A) $a = 65°$, $b = 115°$ and $c = 25°$
(B) $a = 25°$, $b = 75°$ and $c = 65°$
(C) $a = 45°$, $b = 15°$ and $c = 55°$
(D) $a = 65°$, $b = 15°$ and $c = 25°$

25. Two angles of a triangle are of measures 150° and 30°. The third angle will be:

(A) 35°   (B) 75°
(C) 45°   (D) 25°

CONGRUENCE OF TRIANGLES 

7

LEARNING OBJECTIVES

➤ Congruence of Plane Figures
➤ Congruence of Angles
➤ Congruence of Triangles

MULTIPLE CHOICE QUESTIONS

1. What is the side included between the angles A and B in $\triangle ABC$?
   - (A) BC
   - (B) AC
   - (C) None of these
   - (D) AB

2. $\triangle ABC$ and $\triangle PQR$ are congruent under the correspondence: BAC $\leftrightarrow$ RPQ, then the part of $\triangle ABC$ that correspond to PR is
   - (A) BC
   - (B) AB
   - (C) AC
   - (D) None of these

3. $\triangle ABC$ and $\triangle PQR$ are congruent under the correspondence: ABC $\leftrightarrow$ RQP, then the part of $\triangle ABC$ that correspond to $\angle Q$ is
   - (A) $\angle C$
   - (B) $\angle A$
   - (C) $\angle B$
   - (D) None of these

4. $\triangle ABC$ and $\triangle PQR$ are congruent under the correspondence: ABC $\leftrightarrow$ RQP, then the part of $\triangle ABC$ that correspond to $\angle P$ is
   - (A) $\angle B$
   - (B) $\angle A$
   - (C) $\angle C$
   - (D) None of these

5. If $\triangle DEF \cong \triangle ACB$, then the part of $\triangle ACB$ that correspond to $\angle F$ is
   - (A) $\angle B$
   - (B) $\angle A$
   - (C) $\angle C$
   - (D) None of these

6. $\triangle ABC$ and DPQR are congruent under the correspondence: BCA $\leftrightarrow$ RPQ, then the part of $\triangle ABC$ that correspond to PQ is
   - (A) BA
   - (B) CA
   - (C) CB
   - (D) None of these

7. $\triangle ABC$ and $\triangle PQR$ are congruent under the correspondence: ABC $\leftrightarrow$ RPQ, then the part of $\triangle ABC$ that corresponds to PQ is
   - (A) AC
   - (B) AB
   - (C) BC
   - (D) None of these

8. If one angle of a triangle is equal to the sum of the other two angles, then the triangle is
   - (A) An isosceles triangle
   - (B) An obtuse triangle
   - (C) An equilateral triangle
   - (D) A right-angled triangle

9. If two sides of a triangle are 4 cm and 8 cm, then which of the following best describe the length of the third side.
   - (A) 4 < Third side < 8
   - (B) 2 < Third side < 4
   - (C) 4 < Third side < 12
   - (D) 8 < Third side < 12

10. If the largest of an isosceles right-angled triangle is 4 cm. then, the length of the equal sides is
   - (A) $2\sqrt{2}$ cm
   - (B) 4 cm
   - (C) $4\sqrt{2}$ cm
   - (D) 8 cm

11. If three sides of a right-angled triangle are x, y and z such that z is the largest side, then which of the following is correct?

(A) $x^2 + y^2 + z^2 = 0$

(B) $x^2 + y^2 - z^2 = 0$

(C) $x^2 - y^2 + z^2 = 0$

(D) $x^2 - y^2 - z^2 = 0$

12. If a, b and c are sides of a triangle, then which of the following is incorrect?

(A) $a + b = c$

(B) $a + b > c$

(C) $a + c > b$

(D) $b + c > a$

13. If two sides of a triangle are 6 and 8 and the third side is 'x', then which of the following is correct?

(A) $6 < x < 14$

(B) $-2 < x < 14$

(C) $2 < x < 14$

(D) $8 < x < 14$

14. If a, 12, and 13 are the three sides of a right-angled triangle such that 13 is the hypotenuse, then find the value of (A)

(A) 3   (B) 4

(C) 5   (D) 6

15. If for $\triangle ABC$ and $\triangle DEF$, the correspondence CAB$\leftrightarrow$EDF gives a congruence, then which of the following is NOT true?

(A) AC = DE

(B) AB = EF

(C) $\angle A = \angle D$

(D) $\angle C = \angle E$

16. $\triangle ABC \cong \triangle FDE$ and AB = 3 cm, EF = 8 cm and DF = 10 cm. What are the respective lengths of AC and DE in cm?

(A) 10, 3   (B) 10, 8

(C) 8, 3   (D) 3, 10

17. Which of the following is a pair of congruent figures?

(A) A regular pentagon and a regular hexagon.

(B) A rhombus and a square.

(C) Two equilateral triangles of the same length of their sides.

(D) A quadrilateral and a rectangle.

18. In two triangles, the three angles of one triangle are correspondingly equal to three angles of another triangle. Which of the following is a correct statement?

(A) One triangle is an enlarged copy of other.

(B) The two triangles are necessarily congruent.

(C) The two triangles are congruent by A. A. A. congruency criterion.

(D) All of the above.

19. In the given figure, ABC is an isosceles triangle in which AB = AC. If E and F be the midpoints of AC and AB respectively, then BE is equal to _____.

(A) CF   (B) AB

(C) CE   (D) BF

20. Which of the following statements is CORRECT?

(A) In an isosceles triangle, the angles opposite to equal sides are equal.

(B) The bisector of the vertical angle of an isosceles triangle bisects the base at right angles.

(C) If the hypotenuse and an acute angle of one right angled triangle is equal to the hypotenuse and the corresponding acute angle of another triangle, then the triangles are congruent.

(D) All of these

21. In the figure, AD ∥ BCand AD = BC. Then ΔABD ≅ ΔCDB by congruence postulate.

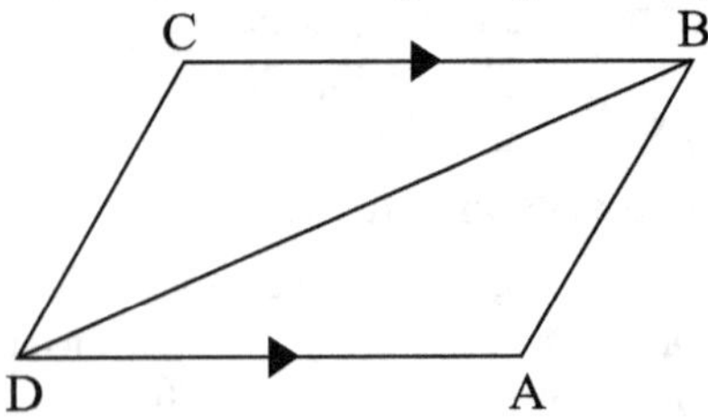

   (A) SSS
   (B) ASA
   (C) AAS
   (D) SAS

22. In ΔABC and ΔDBC, ∠AC = ∠BD and ∠ABC = ∠BCD = 90°. Then ΔABC ≅ ΔDCB by the postulate

   (A) SSS
   (B) SAS
   (C) RHS
   (D) ASA

23. In the given figure, AD = BC, AC = BD. Then ΔPAB is

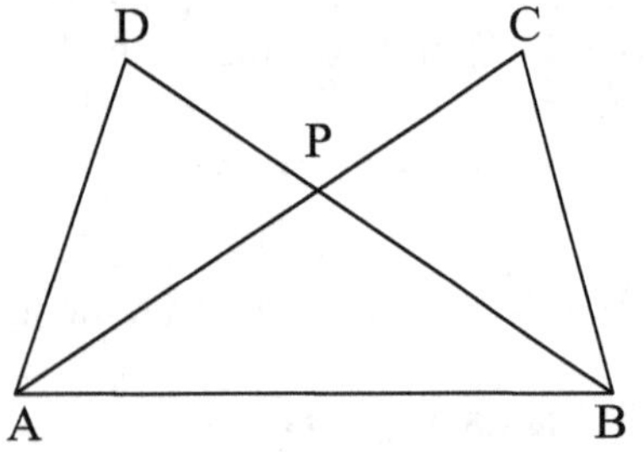

   (A) equilateral
   (B) right angled
   (C) scalene
   (D) isosceles

24. In the figure, PS=QR and PQ=SR, then choose the correct option.

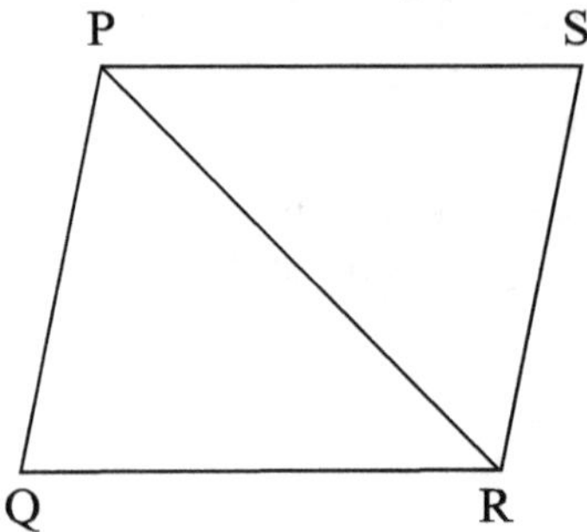

   (A) QRP ≅ PSR
   (B) PQR ≅ PRS
   (C) PQR ≅ RSP
   (D) RQP ≅ RSP

25. The two quadrilaterals are congruent.Which angle in quadrilateral WXYZ corresponds to BCD in quadrilateral ABCD?

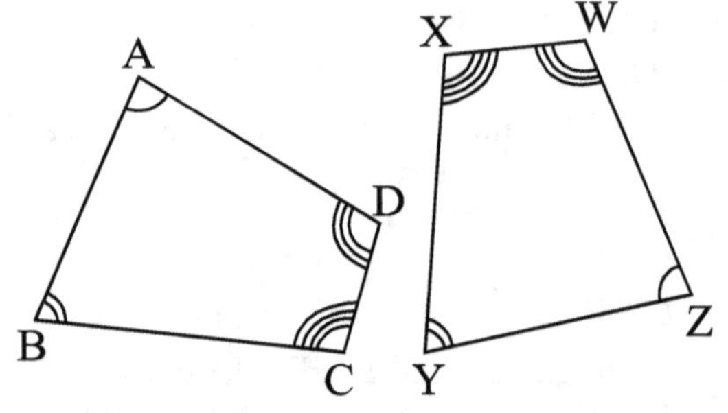

   (A) ∠XYZ
   (B) ∠XWZ
   (C) ∠WZY
   (D) ∠WXY

—Darken Your Choice with HB Pencil—

	A B C D		A B C D		A B C D		A B C D		A B C D
1.	Ⓐ Ⓑ Ⓒ Ⓓ	6.	Ⓐ Ⓑ Ⓒ Ⓓ	11.	Ⓐ Ⓑ Ⓒ Ⓓ	16	Ⓐ Ⓑ Ⓒ Ⓓ	21.	Ⓐ Ⓑ Ⓒ Ⓓ
2.	Ⓐ Ⓑ Ⓒ Ⓓ	7.	Ⓐ Ⓑ Ⓒ Ⓓ	12.	Ⓐ Ⓑ Ⓒ Ⓓ	17.	Ⓐ Ⓑ Ⓒ Ⓓ	22.	Ⓐ Ⓑ Ⓒ Ⓓ
3.	Ⓐ Ⓑ Ⓒ Ⓓ	8.	Ⓐ Ⓑ Ⓒ Ⓓ	13.	Ⓐ Ⓑ Ⓒ Ⓓ	18.	Ⓐ Ⓑ Ⓒ Ⓓ	23.	Ⓐ Ⓑ Ⓒ Ⓓ
4.	Ⓐ Ⓑ Ⓒ Ⓓ	9.	Ⓐ Ⓑ Ⓒ Ⓓ	14.	Ⓐ Ⓑ Ⓒ Ⓓ	19.	Ⓐ Ⓑ Ⓒ Ⓓ	24.	Ⓐ Ⓑ Ⓒ Ⓓ
5.	Ⓐ Ⓑ Ⓒ Ⓓ	10.	Ⓐ Ⓑ Ⓒ Ⓓ	15.	Ⓐ Ⓑ Ⓒ Ⓓ	20.	Ⓐ Ⓑ Ⓒ Ⓓ	25.	Ⓐ Ⓑ Ⓒ Ⓓ

COMPARING QUANTITIES

LEARNING OBJECTIVES

➤ Concept of ratio and percentage
➤ Concept of profit and loss
➤ Calculating discount
➤ Simple interest

MULTIPLE CHOICE QUESTIONS

1. If 20% of $a = b$, then b% of 20 is the same as:
   (A) 4% of a
   (B) 5% of a
   (C) 20% of a
   (D) None of these

2. In a certain school, 20% of students are below 8 years of age. The number of students above 8 years of age is 2/3 of the number of students of 8 years of age which is 48. What is the total number of students in the school?
   (A) 72
   (B) 80
   (C) 120
   (D) 100

3. Two numbers A and B are such that the sum of 5% of A and 4% of B is two-third of the sum of 6% of A and 8% of B. Find the ratio of A : B.
   (A) 2 : 3
   (B) 1 : 1
   (C) 3 : 4
   (D) 4 : 3

4. A student multiplied a number by 3/5 instead of 5/3. What is the percentage error in the calculation?
   (A) 34%
   (B) 44%
   (C) 54%
   (D) 64%

5. In an election between two candidates, one got 55% of the total valid votes, 20% of the votes were invalid. If the total number of votes was 7500, the number of valid votes that the other candidate got, was:
   (A) 2700
   (B) 2900
   (C) 3000
   (D) 3100

6. Three candidates contested an election and received 1136, 7636 and 11628 votes respectively. What percentage of the total votes did the winning candidate get?
   (A) 57%
   (B) 60%
   (C) 65%
   (D) 90%

7. Two tailors X and Y are paid a total of ₹550 per week by their employer. If X is paid 120 percent of the sum paid to Y, how much is Y paid per week?
   (A) ₹200
   (B) ₹250
   (C) ₹300
   (D) None of these

8. Gauri went to the stationers and bought things worth ₹25, out of which 30 paise went on sales tax on taxable purchases. If the tax rate was 6%, then what was the cost of the tax-free items?
   (A) ₹15
   (B) ₹15.70
   (C) ₹19.70
   (D) ₹20

9. Rajeev buys goods worth ₹6650. He gets a rebate of 6% on it. After getting the rebate, he pays sales tax @ 10%. Find the amount he will have to pay for the goods.
   (A) ₹6876.10
   (B) ₹6999.20
   (C) ₹6654
   (D) ₹7000

10. The population of a town increased from 1,75,000 to 2,62,500 in a decade. The average percent increase of population per year is:

(A) 4.37% (B) 5%

(C) 6% (D) 8.75%

11. Alfred buys an old scooter for ₹4700 and spends ₹800 on its repairs. If he sells the scooter for ₹5800, his gain percent is:

(A) $4\dfrac{4}{7}\%$ (B) $5\dfrac{5}{11}\%$

(C) 10% (D) 12%

12. The cost price of 20 articles is the same as the selling price of x articles. If the profit is 25%, then the value of x is:

(A) 15

(B) 16

(C) 18

(D) 25

13. If selling price is doubled, the profit triples. Find the profit percent.

(A) 66%

(B) 100%

(C) 105%

(D) 110%

14. In a certain store, the profit is 320% of the cost. If the cost increases by 25% but the selling price remains constant, approximately what percentage of the selling price is the profit?

(A) 30%

(B) 70%

(C) 100%

(D) 250%

15. A vendor bought toffees at 6 for a rupee. How many for a rupee must he sell to gain 20%?

(A) 3

(B) 4

(C) 5

(D) 6

16. The percentage profit earned by selling an article for ₹1920 is equal to the percentage loss incurred by selling the same article for ₹1280. At what price should the article be sold to make 25% profit?

(A) ₹2000

(B) ₹2200

(C) ₹2400

(D) Data inadequate

17. A shopkeeper expects a gain of 22.5% on his cost price. If in a week, his sale was of ₹392, what was his profit?

(A) ₹18.20 (B) ₹70

(C) ₹72 (D) ₹88.25

18. A man buys a cycle for ₹1400 and sells it at a loss of 15%. What is the selling price of the cycle?

(A) ₹1090

(B) ₹1160

(C) ₹1190

(D) ₹1202

19. Sam purchased 20 dozens of toys at the rate of ₹375 per dozen. He sold each one of them at the rate of ₹33. What was his percentage profit?

(A) 3.5 (B) 4.5

(C) 5.6 (D) 6.5

20. Some articles were bought at 6 articles for ₹5 and sold at 5 articles for ₹6. Gain percent is:

(A) 30%

(B) 33%

(C) 35%

(D) 44%

21. A man wants to sell his scooter. There are two offers, one at ₹12,000 cash and the other a credit of ₹12,880 to be paid after 8 months, money being at 18% per annum. Which is the better offer?

(A) ₹12,000 in cash

(B) ₹12,880 at credit

(C) Both are equally good

(D) None of the above

22. The present worth of ₹1404 due in two equal half-yearly instalments at 8% per annum simple interest is:
   (A) ₹1325
   (B) ₹1300
   (C) ₹1350
   (D) ₹1500

23. If the true discount on a sum due 2 years hence at 14% per annum is ₹168, then the sum due is:
   (A) ₹768
   (B) ₹968
   (C) ₹1960
   (D) ₹2400

24. A sum of money amounts to ₹9800 after 5 years and ₹12005 after 8 years at the same rate of simple interest. The rate of interest per annum is:
   (A) 5%
   (B) 8%
   (C) 12%
   (D) 15%

25. Reena took a loan of ₹1200 with simple interest for as many years as the rate of interest. If she paid ₹432 as interest at the end of the loan period, what was the rate of interest?
   (A) 3.6
   (B) 6
   (C) 18
   (D) Cannot be determined

26. Steve invested $ 10,000 in a savings bank account that earned 2% simple interest. Find the interest earned if the amount was kept in the bank for 4 years.
   (A) $ 500
   (B) $ 650
   (C) $ 775
   (D) $ 800

27. Ryan borrowed $ 15,000 from a bank to buy a car at 10% simple interest. If he paid $ 9,000 as interest while clearing the loan, find the time for which the loan was given.
   (A) 5.5 years
   (B) 6 years
   (C) 8.5 years
   (D) 9 years

28. In what time does a sum of money become four times at the simple interest rate of 5% per annum?
   (A) 40 years
   (B) 45 years
   (C) 60 years
   (D) 80 years

29. The simple interest on ₹1650 will be less than the interest on ₹1800 at 4% simple interest by ₹30. Find the time.
   (A) 3 years
   (B) 5 years
   (C) 7 years
   (D) 9 years

30. Bobby invested a certain sum of money at 8% p.a. simple interest for 'n' years. At the end of 'n' years, Bobby got back 4 times his original investment. What is the value of n?
   (A) 50 years
   (B) 25 years
   (C) 12 years 6 months
   (D) 37 years 6 months

31. An error 2% in excess is made while measuring the side of a square. The percentage of error in the calculated area of the square is:
    (A) 2% (B) 2.02%
    (C) 4% (D) 4.04%

32. A towel, when bleached, was found to have lost 20% of its length and 10% of its breadth. The percentage of decrease in area is:
    (A) 10% (B) 10.08%
    (C) 20% (D) 28%28.

33. A factory makes a profit of ₹1446 on every batch of juice produced and loses ₹106 on every batch because of the juice which gets spilled during production. The factory sold 90 batches of juice in a day. Find the total profit or loss made by the factory.
    (A) Profit of ₹1,20,600
    (B) Loss of ₹1,20,600
    (C) Profit of ₹1,60,200
    (D) Loss of ₹1,60,200

34. A trader owes a merchant ₹10,028 due 1 year hence. The trader wants to settle the account after 3 months. If the rate of interest is 12% per annum, how much cash should he pay?
    (A) ₹9025.20 (B) ₹9200
    (C) ₹9600 (D) ₹9560

35. An automobile financier claims to be lending money at simple interest, but he includes the interest every six months for calculating the principal. If he is charging an interest of 10%, the effective rate of interest becomes:
    (A) 10%
    (B) 10.25%
    (C) 10.5%
    (D) None of these

Darken Your Choice with HB Pencil

1.	Ⓐ	Ⓑ	Ⓒ	Ⓓ	8.	Ⓐ	Ⓑ	Ⓒ	Ⓓ	15.	Ⓐ	Ⓑ	Ⓒ	Ⓓ	22	Ⓐ	Ⓑ	Ⓒ	Ⓓ	29.	Ⓐ	Ⓑ	Ⓒ	Ⓓ
2.	Ⓐ	Ⓑ	Ⓒ	Ⓓ	9.	Ⓐ	Ⓑ	Ⓒ	Ⓓ	16.	Ⓐ	Ⓑ	Ⓒ	Ⓓ	23.	Ⓐ	Ⓑ	Ⓒ	Ⓓ	30.	Ⓐ	Ⓑ	Ⓒ	Ⓓ
3.	Ⓐ	Ⓑ	Ⓒ	Ⓓ	10.	Ⓐ	Ⓑ	Ⓒ	Ⓓ	17.	Ⓐ	Ⓑ	Ⓒ	Ⓓ	24.	Ⓐ	Ⓑ	Ⓒ	Ⓓ	31.	Ⓐ	Ⓑ	Ⓒ	Ⓓ
4.	Ⓐ	Ⓑ	Ⓒ	Ⓓ	11.	Ⓐ	Ⓑ	Ⓒ	Ⓓ	18.	Ⓐ	Ⓑ	Ⓒ	Ⓓ	25.	Ⓐ	Ⓑ	Ⓒ	Ⓓ	32.	Ⓐ	Ⓑ	Ⓒ	Ⓓ
5.	Ⓐ	Ⓑ	Ⓒ	Ⓓ	12.	Ⓐ	Ⓑ	Ⓒ	Ⓓ	19.	Ⓐ	Ⓑ	Ⓒ	Ⓓ	26.	Ⓐ	Ⓑ	Ⓒ	Ⓓ	33.	Ⓐ	Ⓑ	Ⓒ	Ⓓ
6.	Ⓐ	Ⓑ	Ⓒ	Ⓓ	13.	Ⓐ	Ⓑ	Ⓒ	Ⓓ	20.	Ⓐ	Ⓑ	Ⓒ	Ⓓ	27.	Ⓐ	Ⓑ	Ⓒ	Ⓓ	34.	Ⓐ	Ⓑ	Ⓒ	Ⓓ
7.	Ⓐ	Ⓑ	Ⓒ	Ⓓ	14.	Ⓐ	Ⓑ	Ⓒ	Ⓓ	21.	Ⓐ	Ⓑ	Ⓒ	Ⓓ	28.	Ⓐ	Ⓑ	Ⓒ	Ⓓ	35.	Ⓐ	Ⓑ	Ⓒ	Ⓓ

RATIONAL NUMBERS

LEARNING OBJECTIVES

➤ Rational numbers and their properties

➤ Operation on rational numbers

MULTIPLE CHOICE QUESTIONS

1. From a rope 68 m long, pieces of equal size are cut. If length of one piece is $4\frac{1}{4}$ m, find the number of such pieces.
   (A) 13 (B) 14
   (C) 15 (D) 16

2. What should be divided by $\frac{-1}{2}$ to obtain the greatest negative integer?
   (A) $\frac{-1}{2}$ (B) $\frac{1}{2}$
   (C) 1 (D) –1

3. The product of two rational numbers is –10. If one of the numbers is 8, what is the other?
   (A) $\frac{4}{5}$
   (B) $\frac{5}{4}$
   (C) $-\frac{4}{5}$
   (D) $-\frac{5}{4}$

4. The sum of two rational numbers is –7. If one of the numbers is $-\frac{15}{16}$, what is the other?
   (A) $\frac{9}{2}$ (B) $-\frac{9}{2}$
   (C) $\frac{7}{2}$ (D) $-\frac{7}{2}$

5. Find the additive inverse of $\left(\frac{4}{5}+\frac{3}{7}\right)$.
   (A) $\frac{43}{35}$ (B) $-\frac{43}{35}$
   (C) $-\frac{35}{43}$ (D) $\frac{35}{43}$

6. What is the value of $\left(2-\frac{1}{2}-\frac{3}{4}\right)$?
   (A) $\frac{1}{4}$ (B) $\frac{3}{4}$
   (C) $\frac{1}{2}$ (D) $-\frac{3}{4}$

7. What is the simplest form of $\frac{84}{288}$?
   (A) $\frac{7}{12}$ (B) $\frac{7}{48}$
   (C) $\frac{7}{24}$ (D) None of these

8. Which of the following is correct?
   (A) $-\frac{2}{3}>\frac{-4}{3}>\frac{-7}{3}>\frac{-11}{3}$
   (B) $\frac{2}{3}>\frac{4}{3}>\frac{7}{3}$
   (C) $\frac{1}{2}<\frac{1}{3}<\frac{1}{4}<\frac{1}{5}$
   (D) None of these

9. By what rational number is $\dfrac{3}{13}$ multiplied to get -12?

(A) -55 (B) -54
(C) -53 (D) -52

10. Which of the following is incorrect?

(A) $\dfrac{1}{2} > \dfrac{1}{3} > \dfrac{1}{4}$ (B) $\dfrac{2}{5} < \dfrac{4}{5} < 1$

(C) $\dfrac{2}{3} > \dfrac{3}{4} > \dfrac{7}{8}$ (D) $\dfrac{1}{6} < \dfrac{2}{5} < \dfrac{3}{4}$

11. Which rational number is in between 2 and 3?

(A) $\dfrac{8}{3}$ (B) $\dfrac{16}{3}$

(C) $\dfrac{15}{4}$ (D) $\dfrac{11}{3}$

12. The cost of $4\dfrac{1}{2}$ metres of cloth is $₹98\dfrac{3}{4}$. What is the cost of cloth per metre?

(A) $\dfrac{295}{18}$ (B) $\dfrac{395}{18}$

(C) $\dfrac{495}{18}$ (D) None of these

13. What is the simplified value of $\left(\dfrac{3}{55} \times \dfrac{-33}{18}\right) - \left(\dfrac{39}{125} \times \dfrac{-15}{78}\right)$?

(A) $\dfrac{1}{25}$ (B) $\dfrac{1}{50}$

(C) $-\dfrac{1}{50}$ (D) $-\dfrac{1}{25}$

14. What is the reciprocal of $\left[\dfrac{2}{3} \div \dfrac{1}{3} - \dfrac{1}{2} \times \dfrac{1}{2}\right]$?

(A) $\dfrac{4}{7}$ (B) $\dfrac{5}{7}$

(C) $\dfrac{3}{7}$ (D) $\dfrac{-4}{7}$

15. The reciprocal of a rational number is $\dfrac{-7}{9}$. What is that rational number?

(A) $\dfrac{-9}{7}$ (B) $\dfrac{9}{7}$

(C) $\dfrac{7}{9}$ (D) 1

16. The sum of reciprocals of two rational numbers is $\dfrac{7}{4}$. If one of the numbers is $\dfrac{2}{3}$ what is the other?

(A) 2 (B) -4
(C) 4 (D) None of these

17. What is the value of x if $\dfrac{121}{13} = \dfrac{x}{104}$?

(A) 948 (B) 968
(C) 978 (D) 988

18. What result will be obtained when the sum of $\dfrac{65}{12}$ and $\dfrac{8}{3}$ is divided by their difference?

(A) $\dfrac{33}{97}$ (B) $\dfrac{97}{33}$

(C) $\dfrac{31}{97}$ (D) $\dfrac{97}{31}$

19. What is the multiplicative inverse of $\left(\dfrac{2}{3} + \dfrac{3}{4}\right)$?

(A) $\dfrac{12}{17}$ (B) $-\dfrac{12}{17}$

(C) 1 (D) 0

20. The cost of 15 articles is $₹87\dfrac{1}{2}$. What is the cost of one article?

(A) $₹\dfrac{25}{6}$ (B) $₹\dfrac{35}{6}$

(C) $₹\dfrac{37}{6}$ (D) None of these

21. Which one of the following statement is false?
    (A) The product of 10 negative integers and 15 positive integers is always positive
    (B) The product of 15 positive integers and 10 negative integers is always negative
    (C) The product of rational number and its reciprocal is always 1
    (D) If a is reciprocal of p then p will be reciprocal of a

22. Steve has a negative rational number which is reciprocal of itself. If he multiplies the rational number with

$$x = \left[\frac{1}{7} \times 4\frac{3}{5} + 4\frac{3}{5} + 7\frac{3}{5} + 4\frac{9}{17} \div 8\frac{7}{17} \right]$$

then which one of the following is the correct statement?
    (A) When x multiplied by that number product will be reciprocal of x
    (B) When x multiplied by that number product will be additive inverse of x
    (C) x will be $\frac{3}{4}$ times
    (D) x will be doubled

23. Which of the following rational numbers are equal?
    (A) $\left(\frac{-9}{12}\right)$ & $\left(\frac{8}{-12}\right)$ (B) $\left(\frac{-12}{20}\right)$ & $\left(\frac{20}{-25}\right)$
    (C) $\left(\frac{-7}{21}\right)$ & $\left(\frac{3}{-9}\right)$ (D) $\left(\frac{-8}{-14}\right)$ & $\left(\frac{13}{21}\right)$

24. Arrange the following rational numbers in ascending order:

$$\left(\frac{3}{5}\right), \left(\frac{-17}{-30}\right), \left(\frac{8}{-15}\right), \left(\frac{-7}{10}\right)$$

    (A) $\left(-\frac{7}{10}\right) < \left(\frac{8}{-15}\right) < \left(\frac{-17}{30}\right) < \left(\frac{3}{5}\right)$
    (B) $\left(\frac{-17}{30}\right) < \left(\frac{-7}{10}\right) < \left(\frac{8}{-15}\right) < \left(\frac{3}{5}\right)$
    (C) $\left(\frac{8}{-15}\right) < \left(\frac{-7}{10}\right) < \left(\frac{-17}{30}\right) < \left(\frac{3}{5}\right)$
    (D) $\left(\frac{-7}{10}\right) < \left(\frac{-17}{30}\right) < \left(\frac{8}{-15}\right) < \left(\frac{3}{5}\right)$

25. Arrange the following rational numbers in descending order:

$$\left(\frac{7}{8}\right), \left(\frac{64}{16}\right), \left(\frac{39}{-12}\right), \left(\frac{5}{-4}\right), \left(\frac{140}{28}\right)$$

    (A) $\left(\frac{-3}{10}\right) > \left(\frac{7}{-15}\right) > \left(\frac{-11}{20}\right) > \left(\frac{17}{-30}\right)$
    (B) $\left(\frac{7}{-15}\right) > \left(\frac{-3}{10}\right) > \left(\frac{-11}{20}\right) > \left(\frac{17}{-30}\right)$
    (C) $\left(\frac{-11}{20}\right) > \left(\frac{7}{-15}\right) > \left(\frac{-3}{10}\right) > \left(\frac{17}{-30}\right)$
    (D) $\left(\frac{-3}{10}\right) > \left(\frac{7}{-15}\right) > \left(\frac{17}{-30}\right) > \left(\frac{-11}{20}\right)$

Darken Your Choice with HB Pencil

1. Ⓐ Ⓑ Ⓒ Ⓓ	6. Ⓐ Ⓑ Ⓒ Ⓓ	11. Ⓐ Ⓑ Ⓒ Ⓓ	16 Ⓐ Ⓑ Ⓒ Ⓓ	21. Ⓐ Ⓑ Ⓒ Ⓓ
2. Ⓐ Ⓑ Ⓒ Ⓓ	7. Ⓐ Ⓑ Ⓒ Ⓓ	12. Ⓐ Ⓑ Ⓒ Ⓓ	17. Ⓐ Ⓑ Ⓒ Ⓓ	22. Ⓐ Ⓑ Ⓒ Ⓓ
3. Ⓐ Ⓑ Ⓒ Ⓓ	8. Ⓐ Ⓑ Ⓒ Ⓓ	13. Ⓐ Ⓑ Ⓒ Ⓓ	18. Ⓐ Ⓑ Ⓒ Ⓓ	23. Ⓐ Ⓑ Ⓒ Ⓓ
4. Ⓐ Ⓑ Ⓒ Ⓓ	9. Ⓐ Ⓑ Ⓒ Ⓓ	14. Ⓐ Ⓑ Ⓒ Ⓓ	19. Ⓐ Ⓑ Ⓒ Ⓓ	24. Ⓐ Ⓑ Ⓒ Ⓓ
5. Ⓐ Ⓑ Ⓒ Ⓓ	10. Ⓐ Ⓑ Ⓒ Ⓓ	15. Ⓐ Ⓑ Ⓒ Ⓓ	20. Ⓐ Ⓑ Ⓒ Ⓓ	25. Ⓐ Ⓑ Ⓒ Ⓓ

PRACTICAL GEOMETRY

LEARNING OBJECTIVES

➤ Concepts of Practical Geometry

MULTIPLE CHOICE QUESTIONS

1. $\triangle ABC$ is right-angled at C. If AC = 5 cm and BC = 12 cm find the length of AB.
   (A) 13 cm   (B) 7 cm
   (C) 17 cm   (D) None of these

2. In the Pythagoras property, the triangle must be ___________ .
   (A) obtuse-angled   (B) acute-angled
   (C) None of these   (D) right-angled

3. The sum of the lengths of any two sides of a triangle is ___________ the third side of the triangle.
   (A) greater than   (B) double
   (C) less than   (D) half

4. A triangle in which two sides are of equal lengths is called ___________ .
   (A) acute-angled   (B) scalene
   (C) isosceles   (D) equilateral

5. How many altitude can a triangle have?
   (A) 1   (B) 3
   (C) 2   (D) None of these

6. A/an ___________ connect a vertex of a triangle to the mid-point of the opposite side.
   (A) vertex   (B) median
   (C) None of these   (D) altitude

7. How many medians a triangle can have?
   (A) 1   (B) 3
   (C) 2   (D) None of these

8. In any right-angled triangle, the square of the length of hypotenuse is equal to the _____ of the squares of the lengths of the other two sides.
   (A) product
   (B) sum
   (C) difference
   (D) quotient

9. In any right-angled triangle, the square of the length of _______ is equal to the sum of the squares of the lengths of the other two sides.
   (A) hypotenuse
   (B) altitude
   (C) base
   (D) None of these

10. A triangle can be constructed by taking two of its angles as
    (A) 110°, 40°
    (B) 70°, 115°
    (C) 135°, 45°
    (D) 90°, 90°

11. A triangle can be constructed by taking its sides as
    (A) 1.8 cm, 2.6 cm, 4.4 cm
    (B) 2 cm, 3 cm, 4 cm
    (C) 2.4 cm, 2.4 cm, 6.4 cm
    (D) 3.2 cm, 2.3 cm, 5.5 cm

12. Out of the following which is a 3-D figure?
    (A) Square   (B) Sphere
    (C) Triangle   (D) Circle

13. All faces of a pyramid are always
    (A) triangular   (B) rectangular
    (C) congruent   (D) None of these

14. If three cubes each of edge 4 cm are placed end to end, then the dimensions of resulting solid are
    (A) 12 cm × 4 cm × 4 cm
    (B) 4 cm × 8 cm × 4 cm
    (C) 4 cm × 8 cm × 12 cm
    (D) 4 cm × 6 cm × 8 cm

15. A solid that has only one vertex is
    (A) pyramid   (B) cube
    (C) cone   (D) cylinder

16. While constructing a parallel line to a given line, we______.
    (A) copy a segment
    (B) bisect a segment
    (C) copy an angle
    (D) construct a perpendicular

17. Identify the given lines l, m are _________.

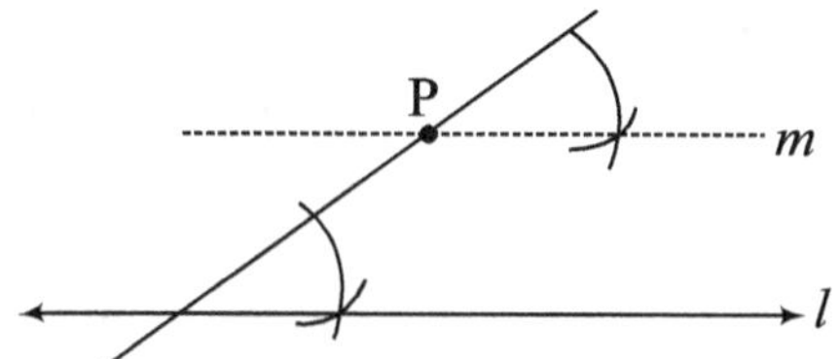

    (A) Parallel
    (B) Perpendicular
    (C) Bisector
    (D) Diagonal

18. Length of sides of a Δ ABC is AB = 5 cm, AC = 3 cm and BC = 4 cm. If the construction of the triangle formed by these three sides include following steps, then answer the following question:

    Which of the following is the last step of construction?

Steps of construction:

Step 1. Now join A to C and B to C.

Step 2. Assuming A a centre draw an arc of radius 3 cm

Step 3. Now assuming B as centre draw an arc of 4 cm intersecting the previous arc at C.

Step 4. Draw a line segment AB = 5cm
    (A) 1   (B) 2
    (C) 3   (D) 4

19. The steps for construction of ΔDEF with DE = 4 cm, EF = 6.5 cm and DF = 8.6 cm are given below in jumbled order:
    1. Draw arcs of length 4 cm from D and 6.5 cm from F and mark the intersection point as E.
    2. Join D-E and F-E.
    3. Draw a line segment of length DF = 8.6 cm.

    The correct order of the steps is:
    (A) 3-1-2   (B) 1-2-3
    (C) 2-3-1   (D) 2-1-3

20. Construct a triangle ABC, in which AB = 5.5 cm, AC = 6.5 cm and ∠BAC = 70°.

    If the steps of construction are given as below the answer the following question:

    Which is the 2nd step of construction?
    1. At A, construct a line segment AE, sufficiently large, such that ∠BAC at 70°, use protractor to measure 70°.
    2. Draw a line segment which is sufficiently long using ruler.
    3. With A as centre and radius 6.5 cm, draw the line cutting AE at C, join BC, then ABC is the required triangle.
    4. Locate points A and B on it such that AB = 5.5 cm.

    (A) 1
    (B) 2
    (C) 3
    (D) none of the above

21. Given *a*, *b* and *c* are sides of a triangle, identify the correctly constructed triangle.

    <u>a</u> <u>b</u> <u>c</u>

    (A)   (B)

    (C)   (D)

22. Construct a $\triangle PQR$ such that $\angle P = 30°$, $\angle Q = 60°$ and $PQ = 10$ cm.

    If following are the steps of construction, then answer the following question:

    Which of the following is the first step of construction?

    Steps of Construction:

    Step 1. At P, draw a ray making an angle of 30°.

    Step 2. At Q, draw another ray making an angle of 60° which intersects the first ray at R. Thus, $\triangle PQR$ is the required triangle.

    Step 3. Draw a line segment PQ = 10cm.

    (A) 1   (B) 2
    (C) 3   (D) none of these

23. Length of sides of a $\triangle ABC$ is AB = 5 cm, AC = 3 cm and BC = 4 cm. Then, construct the triangle formed by these three sides by following these steps. Put them in proper order.

    Step 1. Draw a line segment AB=5 cm

    Step 2. Now assuming B as centre draw an arc of 4 cm intersecting the previous arc at C.

    Step 3. Assuming A a centre draw an arc of radius 3 cm

Step 4. Now join A to C and B to C.

(A) 1-3-2-4   (B) 1-4-2-3
(C) 2-3-4-1   (D) None of these

24. Construct a $\triangle PQR$ such that $\angle P = 30°$, $\angle Q = 60°$ and $PQ = 10$ cm.

    If following are the steps of construction, then which of the following is not a part of construction?

    Steps of Construction:

    i.   Draw a line segment PQ = 10 cm.

    ii. At P, draw a ray making an angle of 30°.

    iii. At Q, draw another ray making an angle of 60° which intersects the first ray at R.

    $\triangle PQR$ is the required triangle.

    (A) 1   (B) 2
    (C) 3   (D) None of these

25. Construct a $\triangle PQR$ such that $\angle P = 30°$, $\angle Q = 60°$ and $PQ = 10$ cm.

    If the following are the steps of construction, then answer the following question:

    Which of the following is the last step of construction?

    Steps of Construction:

    Step 1. At P, draw a ray making an angle of 30°.

    Step 2. At Q, draw another ray making an angle of 60°which intersects the first ray at R. Thus, $\triangle PQR$ is the required triangle.

    Step 3. Draw a line segment PQ = 10cm.

    (A) 1   (B) 2
    (C) 3   (D) None of these

————Darken Your Choice with HB Pencil————

1.	Ⓐ Ⓑ Ⓒ Ⓓ	6.	Ⓐ Ⓑ Ⓒ Ⓓ	11.	Ⓐ Ⓑ Ⓒ Ⓓ	16	Ⓐ Ⓑ Ⓒ Ⓓ	21.	Ⓐ Ⓑ Ⓒ Ⓓ
2.	Ⓐ Ⓑ Ⓒ Ⓓ	7.	Ⓐ Ⓑ Ⓒ Ⓓ	12.	Ⓐ Ⓑ Ⓒ Ⓓ	17.	Ⓐ Ⓑ Ⓒ Ⓓ	22.	Ⓐ Ⓑ Ⓒ Ⓓ
3.	Ⓐ Ⓑ Ⓒ Ⓓ	8.	Ⓐ Ⓑ Ⓒ Ⓓ	13.	Ⓐ Ⓑ Ⓒ Ⓓ	18.	Ⓐ Ⓑ Ⓒ Ⓓ	23.	Ⓐ Ⓑ Ⓒ Ⓓ
4.	Ⓐ Ⓑ Ⓒ Ⓓ	9.	Ⓐ Ⓑ Ⓒ Ⓓ	14.	Ⓐ Ⓑ Ⓒ Ⓓ	19.	Ⓐ Ⓑ Ⓒ Ⓓ	24.	Ⓐ Ⓑ Ⓒ Ⓓ
5.	Ⓐ Ⓑ Ⓒ Ⓓ	10.	Ⓐ Ⓑ Ⓒ Ⓓ	15.	Ⓐ Ⓑ Ⓒ Ⓓ	20.	Ⓐ Ⓑ Ⓒ Ⓓ	25.	Ⓐ Ⓑ Ⓒ Ⓓ

OLYMPIAD WORKBOOK (IMO) CLASS – 7

ELEMENTARY MENSURATION: PERIMETER & AREA

11

LEARNING OBJECTIVES

➤ Fundamental concepts of Triangles

➤ Fundamental concepts of Quadrilaterals

MULTIPLE CHOICE QUESTIONS

1. The diagonal of the floor of a rectangular closet is 7.5 feet. The shorter side of the closet is 4.5 feet. What is the area of the closet in square feet?
   (A) 5   (B) 13
   (C) 27   (D) 37

2. A towel, when bleached, was found to have lost 20% of its length and 10% of its breadth. The percentage of decrease in area is:
   (A) 10%   (B) 10.08%
   (C) 20%   (D) 28%

3. A man walked diagonally across a square plot. Approximately, what is the percent saved by not walking along the edges?
   (A) 20   (B) 24
   (C) 30   (D) 33

4. The diagonal of a rectangle is 41 cm and its area is 20 sq. cm. The perimeter of the rectangle must be:
   (A) 9 cm   (B) 18 cm
   (C) 20 cm   (D) 41 cm

5. What is the least number of squares tiles required to pave the floor of a room 15 m 17 cm long and 9 m 2 cm broad?
   (A) 814   (B) 820
   (C) 840   (D) 844

6. The difference between the length and breadth of a rectangle is 23 m. If its perimeter is 206 m, then its area is:
   (A) 1520 m²   (B) 2420 m²
   (C) 2480 m²   (D) 2520 m²

7. The length of a rectangle is halved, while its breadth is tripled. What is the percentage change in area?
   (A) 25% increase   (B) 50% increase
   (C) 50% decrease   (D) 75% decrease

8. The length of a rectangular plot is 20 metres more than its breadth. If the cost of fencing the plot @ 26.50 per metre is ₹5300, what is the length of the plot in metres?
   (A) 40   (B) 50
   (C) 120   (D) None of these

9. A rectangular field is to be fenced on three sides leaving a side of 20 feet uncovered. If the area of the field is 680 sq. feet, how many feet of fencing will be required?
   (A) 34   (B) 40
   (C) 68   (D) 88

10. A tank is 25 m long, 12 m wide and 6 m deep. The cost of plastering its walls and bottom at 75 paise per sq. m, is:
    (A) ₹456   (B) ₹458
    (C) ₹558   (D) ₹568

11. The area of playground is 1600 m². What is the perimeter?

I. It is a perfect square playground.

II. It costs ₹3200 to put a fence around the playground at the rate of ₹20 per metre.

(A) I alone sufficient while II alone not sufficient to answer

(B) II alone sufficient while I alone not sufficient to answer

(C) Either I or II alone sufficient to answer

(D) Both I and II are not sufficient to answer

12. The area of a rectangle is equal to the area of a right-angled triangle. What is the length of the rectangle?

I. The base of the triangle is 40 cm.

II. The height of the triangle is 50 cm.

(A) I alone sufficient while II alone not sufficient to answer

(B) II alone sufficient while I alone not sufficient to answer

(C) Either I or II alone sufficient to answer

(D) Both I and II are not sufficient to answer

13. What is the height of the triangle?

I. The area of the triangle is 20 times its base.

II. The perimeter of the triangle is equal to the perimeter of a square of side 10 cm.

(A) I alone sufficient while II alone not sufficient to answer

(B) II alone sufficient while I alone not sufficient to answer

(C) Either I or II alone sufficient to answer

(D) Both I and II are not sufficient to answer

14. What will be the cost of painting the inner walls of a room if the rate of painting is ₹20 per square foot?

I. Circumference of the floor is 44 feet.

II. The height of the wall of the room is 12 feet.

(A) I alone sufficient while II alone not sufficient to answer

(B) II alone sufficient while I alone not sufficient to answer

(C) Either I or II alone sufficient to answer

(D) Both I and II are necessary to answer

15. What is the area of the hall?

I. Material cost of flooring per square metre is ₹2.50.

II. Labour cost of flooring the hall is ₹3500.

III. Total cost of flooring the hall is ₹14,500.

(A) I and II only

(B) II and III only

(C) All I, II and III

(D) Any two of the three

16. What is the area of a right-angled triangle?

I. The perimeter of the triangle is 30 cm.

II. The ratio between the base and the height of the triangle is 5 : 12.

III. The area of the triangle is equal to the area of a rectangle of length 10 cm.

(A) I and II only

(B) II and III only

(C) I and III only

(D) III, and either I or II only

17. What is the area of rectangular field?

I. The perimeter of the field is 110 metres.

II. The length is 5 metres more than the width.

III. The ratio between length and width is 6 : 5 respectively.

(A) I and II only

(B) Any two of the three

(C) All I, II and III

(D) I, and either II or III only

18. What is the area of the given rectangle?

I. Perimeter of the rectangle is 60 cm.

II. Breadth of the rectangle is 12 cm.

III. Sum of two adjacent sides is 30 cm.

(A) I only

(B) II only

(C) I and II only

(D) II and either I or III

19. What is the cost of painting the two adjacent walls of a hall at ₹5 per m², which has no windows or doors?

I. The area of the hall is 24 sq. m.

II. The breadth, length and height of the hall are in the ratio of 4 : 6 : 5 respectively.

III. Area of one wall is 30 sq. m.

(A) I only

(B) II only

(C) III only

(D) Both I and II

20. Find the area of the largest circle that can be drawn in a square of side 14 cm.

(A) 154 cm^2

(B) 144 cm^2

(C) 136 cm^2

(D) 121 cm^2

21. In a quadrilateral, the length of one of its diagonal is 23 cm and the perpendiculars drawn on this diagonal from other two vertices measure 17 cm and 7 cm respectively. Find the area of the quadrilateral.

(A) 225 cm^2

(B) 149 cm^2

(C) 276 cm^2

(D) 136 cm^2

22. The circumference of a circle is 100 cm. Find the side of the square inscribed in the circle.

(A) $\sqrt{2} \times \dfrac{50}{\pi}$

(B) $\sqrt{2} \times \dfrac{60}{\pi}$

(C) $\sqrt{3} \times \dfrac{60}{\pi}$

(D) $\sqrt{3} \times \dfrac{30}{\pi}$

23. If the radius of a circle is increased by 5%, find the percentage increase in its area.

(A) 10%

(B) 10.25%

(C) 10.75%

(D) 11%

24. If all sides of a hexagon is increased by 2%, find the percentage increase in its area.

(A) 6.06%

(B) 4.04%

(C) 10.05%

(D) 5.80%

25. If diameter of a circle is increased by 12%, find the percentage increase in its circumference.

(A) 6%　　(B) 12%

(C) 18%　　(D) 9%

HOTS (ACHIEVERS SECTION)

26. The area of playground is 1600 m^2. What is the perimeter?

I. It is a perfect square playground.

II. It costs ₹3200 to put a fence around the playground at the rate of ₹20 per metre.

(A) I alone sufficient while II alone not sufficient to answer

(B) II alone sufficient while I alone not sufficient to answer

(C) Either I or II alone sufficient to answer

(D) Both I and II are not sufficient to answer

27. The area of a rectangle is equal to the area of a right-angled triangle. What is the length of the rectangle?

I. The base of the triangle is 40 cm.

II. The height of the triangle is 50 cm.

(A) I alone sufficient while II alone not sufficient to answer

(B) II alone sufficient while I alone not sufficient to answer

(C) Either I or II alone sufficient to answer

(D) Both I and II are not sufficient to answer

28. What is the height of the triangle?

I. The area of the triangle is 20 times its base.

II. The perimeter of the triangle is equal to the perimeter of a square of side 10 cm.

(A) I alone sufficient while II alone not sufficient to answer

(B) II alone sufficient while I alone not sufficient to answer

(C) Either I or II alone sufficient to answer

(D) Both I and II are not sufficient to answer

29. What will be the cost of painting the inner walls of a room if the rate of painting is ₹20 per square foot?

I. Circumference of the floor is 44 feet.

II. The height of the wall of the room is 12 feet.

(A) I alone sufficient while II alone not sufficient to answer

(B) II alone sufficient while I alone not sufficient to answer

(C) Either I or II alone sufficient to answer

(D) Both I and II are necessary to answer

30. What is the area of the hall?

I. Material cost of flooring per square metre is ₹2.50.

II. Labour cost of flooring the hall is ₹3500.

III. Total cost of flooring the hall is ₹14,500.

(A) I and II only

(B) II and III only

(C) All I, II and III

(D) Any two of the three

---Darken Your Choice with HB Pencil---

1. Ⓐ Ⓑ Ⓒ Ⓓ	7. Ⓐ Ⓑ Ⓒ Ⓓ	13. Ⓐ Ⓑ Ⓒ Ⓓ	19 Ⓐ Ⓑ Ⓒ Ⓓ	25. Ⓐ Ⓑ Ⓒ Ⓓ
2. Ⓐ Ⓑ Ⓒ Ⓓ	8. Ⓐ Ⓑ Ⓒ Ⓓ	14. Ⓐ Ⓑ Ⓒ Ⓓ	20. Ⓐ Ⓑ Ⓒ Ⓓ	26. Ⓐ Ⓑ Ⓒ Ⓓ
3. Ⓐ Ⓑ Ⓒ Ⓓ	9. Ⓐ Ⓑ Ⓒ Ⓓ	15. Ⓐ Ⓑ Ⓒ Ⓓ	21. Ⓐ Ⓑ Ⓒ Ⓓ	27. Ⓐ Ⓑ Ⓒ Ⓓ
4. Ⓐ Ⓑ Ⓒ Ⓓ	10. Ⓐ Ⓑ Ⓒ Ⓓ	16. Ⓐ Ⓑ Ⓒ Ⓓ	22. Ⓐ Ⓑ Ⓒ Ⓓ	28. Ⓐ Ⓑ Ⓒ Ⓓ
5. Ⓐ Ⓑ Ⓒ Ⓓ	11. Ⓐ Ⓑ Ⓒ Ⓓ	17. Ⓐ Ⓑ Ⓒ Ⓓ	23. Ⓐ Ⓑ Ⓒ Ⓓ	29. Ⓐ Ⓑ Ⓒ Ⓓ
6. Ⓐ Ⓑ Ⓒ Ⓓ	12. Ⓐ Ⓑ Ⓒ Ⓓ	18. Ⓐ Ⓑ Ⓒ Ⓓ	24. Ⓐ Ⓑ Ⓒ Ⓓ	30. Ⓐ Ⓑ Ⓒ Ⓓ

ALGEBRAIC EXPRESSIONS

12

LEARNING OBJECTIVES

➤ Concept of algebraic expressions

MULTIPLE CHOICE QUESTIONS

1. What is the product of $-3m^2np$, $\dfrac{1}{3}nm^3p^2$ and $\dfrac{2}{3}m^2n^2p^2$?

   (A) $-\dfrac{1}{3}m^5n^4p^4$ (B) $-\dfrac{2}{3}m^7n^4p^4$

   (C) $-\dfrac{2}{3}m^7n^4p^5$ (D) $-\dfrac{2}{3}m^6n^3p^6$

2. What is the product of $-xyz^2$, $-2yx^2z$ and $\dfrac{1}{2}x^3yz$?

   (A) $x^6y^3z^4$ (B) $x^6y^2z^3$
   (C) $x^6y^3z^3$ (D) $x^6y^2z^2$

3. $5 - (3x + 2y) - 3(x - y) + 7x + y =?$
   (A) $x + 2y + 5$ (B) $x - 2y + 5$
   (C) $2x + 2y + 5$ (D) None of these

4. Find the product of the sum of $3x^2 + 5y^2$ and $x^2 - 4y^2$ and the difference of $(x^2 - y^2)$ and $2x^2 + 3y^2$.
   (A) $4x^4 - 16x^2y^2 + 4y^4$
   (B) $4x^4 + 17x^2y^2 + 4y^4$
   (C) $4x^4 - 15x^2y^2 + 4y^4$
   (D) None of these

5. Find the value of $(2.3a^5b^2) \times (1.2a^2b^2)$ when $a = 1$ and $b = 0.5$.

   (A) 0.10725
   (B) 0.1275
   (C) 0.1525
   (D) 0.1725

6. Find the value of $(2.6\ m^2n) \times (5mn^2)$ when $m = \dfrac{1}{2}$ and $n = \dfrac{1}{3}$.

   (A) $\dfrac{13}{162}$ (B) $\dfrac{13}{216}$

   (C) $\dfrac{3}{216}$ (D) $\dfrac{130}{216}$

7. Find the product of ab^2c, $-a^2bc^2$, $-abc^3$ and $-a^2bc$.
   (A) $-a^6b^5c^7$
   (B) $a^6b^6c^7$
   (C) $-a^6b^6c^5$
   (D) $-a^5b^5c^5$

8. What is obtained when $(3x - \dfrac{4}{5}xy^2)$ is multiplied by $\dfrac{1}{3}xy$?

   (A) $x^2y^2 - \dfrac{4}{15}x^2y^3$

   (B) $x^2y - \dfrac{4}{15}x^2y^3$

   (C) $xy^2 - \dfrac{4}{15}xy^2$

   (D) None of these

9. Find the numerical value of the product $3s(s^2 - st)$ when $s = 2$ and $t = 5$.
   (A) -32 (B) -36
   (C) -38 (D) None of these

10. What is the simplified value of $a(b - c) + b(c - a) + c(a - b)$?
   (A) 0   (B) 1
   (C) -1 (D) None of these

11. Simplify $a(b - 2c) + 2b(c - 2a) + c\,(3a - 2b)$.
   (A) $2ab - ac$ (B) $ab - ac$
   (C) $ac - 3ab$ (D) $ab - 3ab$

12. What is the product of $-3x^2y^2z^2$ and $-5xy^2z$
   (A) $15\,x^2y^2z^2$ (B) $15\,x^3y^2z^2$
   (C) $15\,x^3y^3z^3$ (D) $15\,x^3y^4z^3$

13. Find the simplest expression of
   $a(b - c) - b(c - 2a) - c\,(2a - b)$
   (A) $3ab - ac$ (B) $3a(b - c)$
   (C) $2(ab - ac)$ (D) $2ab - 3ac$

14. What is product of $(x^4 - \dfrac{1}{x^4})$ and $(x + \dfrac{1}{x})$?

   (A) $x^5 + x^3 - \dfrac{1}{x^3} - \dfrac{1}{x^5}$

   (B) $x^5 + x^4 - \dfrac{1}{x^4} - \dfrac{1}{x^5}$

   (C) $x^5 + x^3 - \dfrac{1}{x^4} - \dfrac{1}{x^5}$

   (D) None of these

15. What is the product of $(x^3 + y^3)$ and $(x^2 - y^2)$?
   (A) $x^5 + x^3y^2 - x^2y^3 - y^5$
   (B) $x^5 - x^3y^2 + x^2y^3 - y^5$
   (C) $x^5 - x^2y^2 + x^3y^3 - y^5$
   (D) None of these

16. Find the difference of $x^2 - xy + y^2 + yz$ and $2x^2 - 3xy - y^2 - yz$.
   (A) $x^2 - 2xy - 2y^2 - 2yz$
   (B) $x^2 + 2xy + 2y^2 - 2yz$
   (C) $x^2 - 2xy - y^2 + 2yz$
   (D) None of these

17. What is the result when the sum of $(-5x^2 + 7xy + 2y^2)$ and $(x^2 - 3xy - y^2)$ is subtracted from -7?
   (A) $4x^2 - 4xy + y^2 + 7$
   (B) $4x^2 - 4xy - y^2 - 7$
   (C) $4x^2 - xy + y^2 + 7$
   (D) $4x^2 + 4xy - 4y^2 - 7$

18. What is the product of $(0.8m - 0.7n)$ and $(1.5n - 1.7m)$?
   (A) $2.39\,mn - 1.05\,n^2 - 1.36\,m^2$
   (B) $1.19\,mn - 1.15\,n^2 + 1.36\,m^2$
   (C) $1.39\,mn - 1.05\,n^2 + 1.36\,m^2$
   (D) None of these

19. Find the sum of $0.3x^2 - 3xy + 0.8y^2$ and $4x^2 - 2y^2 + 0.7xy$?
   (A) $4.3x^2 - 1.3xy + 1.2\,y^2$
   (B) $4.3x^2 - 2.3xy + 1.2\,y^2$
   (C) $4.3x^2 - 2.3xy - 1.2\,y^2$
   (D) None of these

20. Find the product of $(7x^2 - x + 11)$ and $(x^2 - 3)$.
   (A) $7x^4 - x^3 - 10x^2 + 3x - 33$
   (B) $7x^4 + x^3 - 21x^2 + 3x - 33$
   (C) $7x^4 - x^3 + 11x^2 - 3x - 33$
   (D) None of these

21. What is the product of $1.5\,a(10a^2b - 100ab^2)$
   (A) $15a^3b - 150a^2b^2$
   (B) $15a^2b - 1500a^2b^2$
   (C) $150a^3b - 150a^2b^2$
   (D) None of these

22. Find the simplified expression of
   $7x^2 - [x^2 - 3x - \{x + y\}] - (5x - 3y + 3)$.
   (A) $6x^2 - 2x + 4y + 3$
   (B) $6x^2 - x + 4y - 3$
   (C) $6x^2 - 2x - 4y - 3$
   (D) None of these

23. Find the result of
   $x(x + 4) + 3x\,(2x^2 - 3) + 4x^2 + 5$?
   (A) $6x^3 + 5x^2 - 13x + 5$
   (B) $6x^3 + 4x^2 - 5x + 5$
   (C) $6x^3 + 5x^2 - 5x + 5$
   (D) None of these

24. $4mn\,(m-n) - 6m^2\,(n-n^2) - 3n^2(2m^2-m) = ?$
   (A) $2m^2n - n^2m$
   (B) $-mn\,(2m-n)$
   (C) $m^2n - 2n^2m$
   (D) $-mn\,(2m+n)$

25. $a^2b(a-b^2) - ab^2\,(3ab-a^2) - a^3b\,(1-2b) = ?$
   (A) $3a^3b^2 - 4a^2b^3$
   (B) $3a^3b^2 - 3a^2b^3$
   (C) $a^3b^2 - 4a^2b^3$
   (D) $3a^3b^2 + 4a^2b^3$

HOTS (ACHIEVERS SECTION)

26. What should be added to $xy - 3yz + 4zx$ to get $4xy - 3zx + 4yz + 7$?
   (A) $3xy - 7zx + 7yz + 7$
   (B) $3xy - 4zx + 7yz + 7$
   (C) $3xy - 2zx + 5yz + 7$
   (D) $3xy - 7zx + 1yz + 7$

27. What should be subtracted from $x^2 - xy + y^2 - x + y + 3$ to obtain $-x^2 + 3y^2 - 4xy + 1$?
   (A) $2x^2 + 3xy - 2y^2 - x + y + 2$
   (B) $2x^2 + xy - 2y^2 - x + y + 2$
   (C) $2x^2 + 5xy - 2y^2 - x + y$
   (D) $x^2 + 3xy - 2y^2 - x + y + 2$

28. How much is $x^2 - 2xy + 3y^2$ less than $2x^2 - 3y^2 + xy$?
   (A) $x^2 - 6y^2 + 3xy$ (B) $x^2 - 9y^2 + 3xy$
   (C) $4x^2 - y^2 + 3xy$ (D) $6x^2 - 6y^2 + xy$

29. How much does $a^2 - 3ab + 2b^2$ exceed $2a^2 - 7ab + 9b^2$?
   (A) $5a^2 + ab - 7b^2$
   (B) $a^2 + 4ab - 7b^2$
   (C) $2a^2 + 4ab - 7b^2$
   (D) $7a^2 - 4ab - 7b^2$

30. If $P = a^2 - b^2 + 2ab$, $Q = a^2 + 4b^2 - 6ab$, $R = b^2 + b$, $S = a^2 - 4ab$ and $T = -2a^2 + b^2 - ab + a$. Find $P + Q + R + S - T$.
   (A) $5a^2 + b^2 - 6ab - a + b$
   (B) $a^2 + 3b^2 - 7ab - 7a + b$
   (C) $5a^2 + 3b^2 - 7ab - a + b$
   (D) $5a^2 + 3b^2 - 7ab - a - b$

1.	Ⓐ Ⓑ Ⓒ Ⓓ	7.	Ⓐ Ⓑ Ⓒ Ⓓ	13.	Ⓐ Ⓑ Ⓒ Ⓓ	19	Ⓐ Ⓑ Ⓒ Ⓓ	25.	Ⓐ Ⓑ Ⓒ Ⓓ
2.	Ⓐ Ⓑ Ⓒ Ⓓ	8.	Ⓐ Ⓑ Ⓒ Ⓓ	14.	Ⓐ Ⓑ Ⓒ Ⓓ	20.	Ⓐ Ⓑ Ⓒ Ⓓ	26.	Ⓐ Ⓑ Ⓒ Ⓓ
3.	Ⓐ Ⓑ Ⓒ Ⓓ	9.	Ⓐ Ⓑ Ⓒ Ⓓ	15.	Ⓐ Ⓑ Ⓒ Ⓓ	21.	Ⓐ Ⓑ Ⓒ Ⓓ	27.	Ⓐ Ⓑ Ⓒ Ⓓ
4.	Ⓐ Ⓑ Ⓒ Ⓓ	10.	Ⓐ Ⓑ Ⓒ Ⓓ	16.	Ⓐ Ⓑ Ⓒ Ⓓ	22.	Ⓐ Ⓑ Ⓒ Ⓓ	28.	Ⓐ Ⓑ Ⓒ Ⓓ
5.	Ⓐ Ⓑ Ⓒ Ⓓ	11.	Ⓐ Ⓑ Ⓒ Ⓓ	17.	Ⓐ Ⓑ Ⓒ Ⓓ	23.	Ⓐ Ⓑ Ⓒ Ⓓ	29.	Ⓐ Ⓑ Ⓒ Ⓓ
6.	Ⓐ Ⓑ Ⓒ Ⓓ	12.	Ⓐ Ⓑ Ⓒ Ⓓ	18.	Ⓐ Ⓑ Ⓒ Ⓓ	24.	Ⓐ Ⓑ Ⓒ Ⓓ	30.	Ⓐ Ⓑ Ⓒ Ⓓ

LEARNING OBJECTIVES

➤ Irrational Numbers

➤ Laws of exponents

MULTIPLE CHOICE QUESTIONS

1. If $(25)^{7.5} \times (5)^{2.5} \div (125)^{1.5} = 5^x$ then $x = ?$
   (A) 8.5   (B) 13
   (C) 16   (D) 17.5

2. $(0.04)^{-1.5} = ?$
   (A) 25   (B) 125
   (C) 250   (D) 625

3. If $3^{(x-y)} = 27$ and $3^{(x+y)} = 243$, then x is equal to:
   (A) 0   (B) 2
   (C) 4   (D) 6

4. If $5^a = 3125$, then the value of $5^{(a-3)}$ is:
   (A) 25   (B) 125
   (C) 625   (D) 1625

5. Given that $10^{0.48} = x$, $10^{0.70} = y$ and $x^z = y^2$, then the value of z is close to:
   (A) 1.45   (B) 1.88
   (C) 2.9   (D) 3.7

6. $(17)^{3.5} \times (17)^? = 17^8$
   (A) 2.29   (B) 2.75
   (C) 4.25   (D) 4.5

7. Find the value of $\sqrt{300}$.
   (A) 15.36   (B) 30
   (C) 9   (D) 17.32

8. Evaluate: $\sqrt{75} + \sqrt{147} = ?$
   (A) 20.7846   (B) 22.3698
   (C) 18.336   (D) 21.7586

9. Find the value of:
   $$\sqrt{80} + 3\sqrt{245} - \sqrt{125} = ?$$
   (A) 38.6395   (B) 44.7214
   (C) 50.2136   (D) 3.2365

10. Find $\sqrt{242} \div \sqrt{72}$.
    (A) 1.2   (B) 2
    (C) $\dfrac{4}{5}$ (D) $1\dfrac{5}{6}$

11. $(18a^8b^6) \div (3a^2b^2)$ simplifies to
    (A) $6a^4b^3$ (B) $6a^{10}b^8$
    (C) $6a^6b^4$ (D) $15a^6b^3$

12. Replace question mark with the suitable answer:
    $$56 - 45 - \sqrt{?} = \sqrt{36}$$
    (A) 25   (B) 35
    (C) 15   (D) 5

13. Replace question mark with the suitable answer:
    $$(?)^2 = \dfrac{4}{25}$$
    (A) 1   (B) 1.5
    (C) 2/5   (D) 3

14. Find $\sqrt{210\dfrac{1}{4}} = ?$
    (A) $13\dfrac{1}{2}$ (B) $15\dfrac{1}{2}$
    (C) $14\dfrac{1}{2}$ (D) $17\dfrac{1}{2}$

15. What is the value of $(0.003)^3$?
    (A) 0.09
    (B) 0.000000027
    (C) 0.00027
    (D) 0.27

16. The value of $\dfrac{10^{22}+10^{20}}{10^{20}}$ is
    (A) 10
    (B) 10^{42}
    (C) 101
    (D) 10^{22}

17. The standard form of the number 12345 is
    (A) 1234.5×10^1
    (B) 123.45×10^2
    (C) 12.345×10^3
    (D) 1.2345×10^4

18. If $2^{1998} - 2^{1997} - 2^{1996} + 2^{1995} = k.2^{1995}$, then the value of k is
    (A) 1
    (B) 2
    (C) 3
    (D) 4

19. Which of the following is equal to 1?
    (A) $2^\circ + 3^\circ + 4^\circ$
    (B) $2^\circ \times 3^\circ \times 4^\circ$
    (C) $(3^\circ - 2^\circ) \times 4^\circ$
    (D) $(3^\circ - 2^\circ) \times (3^\circ + 2^\circ)$

20. Which of the following is not equal to $\left(\dfrac{-5}{4}\right)^4$?
    (A) $\dfrac{(-5)^4}{4^4}$
    (B) $\dfrac{5^4}{(-4)^4}$
    (C) $-\dfrac{5^4}{4^4}$
    (D) $\left(-\dfrac{5}{4}\right) \times \left(-\dfrac{5}{4}\right) \times \left(-\dfrac{5}{4}\right) \times \left(-\dfrac{5}{4}\right)$

HOTS (ACHIEVERS SECTION)

21. If you express 450 as a product of powers of their prime factors, it will be:
    (A) $3 \times 2^2 \times 5^2$
    (B) $2 \times 4^2 \times 5^2$
    (C) $2 \times 3^2 \times 5^2$
    (D) $1 \times 3^2 \times 5^2$

22. If you express 24000 as a product of powers of their prime factors, it will be:
    (A) $6^6 \times 3 \times 2^3$
    (B) $4^6 \times 3 \times 5^3$
    (C) $1 \times 3 \times 5^3$
    (D) $2^6 \times 3 \times 5^3$

23. Correct value of $\left(\dfrac{-1}{2}\right)^2 \times 2^3 \times \left(\dfrac{3}{4}\right)^2$:
    (A) $\dfrac{9}{8}$
    (B) $\dfrac{4}{7}$
    (C) $\dfrac{8}{9}$
    (D) $\dfrac{1}{16}$

24. Correct value of $\left(\dfrac{-1}{2}\right)^2 \times 2^3 \times \left(\dfrac{3}{4}\right)^2$:
    (A) $\dfrac{24}{12225}$
    (B) $\dfrac{14}{16225}$
    (C) $\dfrac{64}{18225}$
    (D) $\dfrac{34}{18225}$

25. If $a = 2$ and $b = 3$, the value of $\left(\left(\dfrac{a}{b}\right) + \left(\dfrac{b}{a}\right)\right)^a$
    (A) $\dfrac{129}{36}$
    (B) $\dfrac{169}{36}$
    (C) $\dfrac{139}{36}$
    (D) $\dfrac{169}{26}$

Darken Your Choice with HB Pencil

1.	(A) (B) (C) (D)	6.	(A) (B) (C) (D)	11.	(A) (B) (C) (D)	16	(A) (B) (C) (D)	21.	(A) (B) (C) (D)
2.	(A) (B) (C) (D)	7.	(A) (B) (C) (D)	12.	(A) (B) (C) (D)	17.	(A) (B) (C) (D)	22.	(A) (B) (C) (D)
3.	(A) (B) (C) (D)	8.	(A) (B) (C) (D)	13.	(A) (B) (C) (D)	18.	(A) (B) (C) (D)	23.	(A) (B) (C) (D)
4.	(A) (B) (C) (D)	9.	(A) (B) (C) (D)	14.	(A) (B) (C) (D)	19.	(A) (B) (C) (D)	24.	(A) (B) (C) (D)
5.	(A) (B) (C) (D)	10.	(A) (B) (C) (D)	15.	(A) (B) (C) (D)	20.	(A) (B) (C) (D)	25.	(A) (B) (C) (D)

SYMMETRY

LEARNING OBJECTIVES

➤ Concept of Symmetry

MULTIPLE CHOICE QUESTIONS

1. How many lines of symmetries are there in regular pentagon?
   (A) 4   (B) 3
   (C) 2   (D) 5

2. How many lines of symmetries are there in a rhombus?
   (A) 1   (B) 4
   (C) 2   (D) 3

3. How many lines of symmetries are there in an isosceles triangle ?
   (A) 3   (B) 2
   (C) 1   (D) None of these

4. Which of the English alphabets has a rotational symmetry of order 0?
   (A) H   (B) A
   (C) I   (D) N

5. A windmill has four blades and rotational symmetry of the order 2×K, Find K
   (A) 1   (B) 2
   (C) 3   (D) 3

6. Which of these has 3 lines of symmetry?
   (A) Any triangle.
   (B) An isosceles triangle.
   (C) An equilateral triangle.
   (D) A right angled triangle.

7. How many of the following letters have rotational symmetry of order more than 1?
   R, B, F, H. O, R S, W, X, Z. N
   (A) 4   (B) 9
   (C) 9   (D) 8

8. Which of the following statements is correct?
   (A) An equilateral triangle has three lines of symmetry.
   (B) A rectangle has four lines of symmetry.
   (C) A circle has only one line of symmetry.
   (D) A parallelogram has two lines of symmetry.

9. Which of the following alphabets has no line of symmetry?
   (A) A   (B) B
   (C) P   (D) O

10. The order of rotational symmetry in the figure given below is

    (A) 4   (B) 2
    (C) 1   (D) Infinitely many

11. Which of the following statements is/are true?

(i) 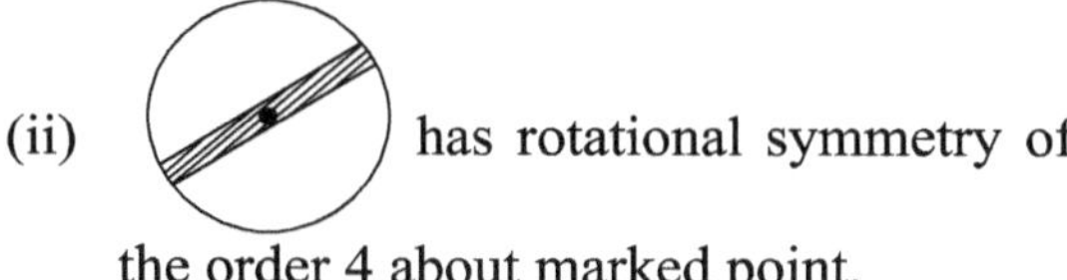 has rotational symmetry of the order 3 about marked point.

(ii)  has rotational symmetry of the order 4 about marked point.

(A) Both (i) and (ii) are true
(B) Only (i) is true
(C) Only (ii) is true
(D) Neither (i) nor (ii) is true

12. How many letters of the English alphabet have at least one line of symmetry?
(A) 14
(B) 15
(C) 12
(D) 13

13. What is the order of rotational symmetry of the given figure?

(A) 0
(B) 1
(C) 2
(D) 4

14. Which of the following shapes has four lines of symmetry?
(A) Rectangle
(B) Rhombus
(C) Square
(D) Both rhombus and square

15. A square is symmetrical about
(A) each of its diagonals
(B) the line joining the midpoints of its opposite sides
(C) both (A) and (B)
(D) none of these

16. How many lines of symmetry does an n-sided regular polygon have?
(A) n
(B) $n-1$
(C) $n+1$
(D) 0

17. What is the product of number of lines of symmetry and order of rotational symmetry of a regular octagon?
(A) 64
(B) 32
(C) 56
(D) 16

18. What is the order of rotation of a circle rotated about its centre?
(A) 0
(B) 1
(C) 4
(D) Infinity

19. How many minimum squares must be shaded to make the given figure symmetrical?

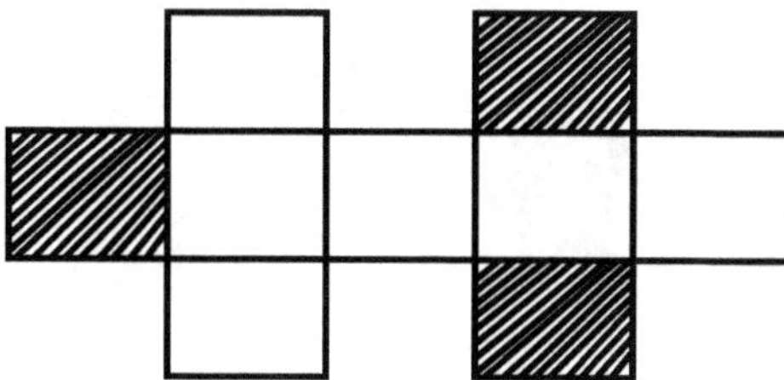

(A) 3
(B) 1
(C) 4
(D) 2

20. What is the order of rotational symmetry of a regular heptagon?
(A) 0
(B) 5
(C) 6
(D) 7

21. Which of the following letters have reflection line of symmetry about vertical mirror?
    (A) B
    (B) V
    (C) C
    (D) Q

22. How many lines of symmetries are there in rectangle?
    (A) 1
    (B) 2
    (C) 0
    (D) None of these

23. How many lines of symmetries are there in a square?
    (A) 3
    (B) 1
    (C) 4
    (D) 2

24. Find the number of lines of symmetry in regular hexagon.
    (A) 4
    (B) 7
    (C) 5
    (D) 6

25. Which of the followings has both horizontal as well as vertical line of symmetry?
    (A) S
    (B) H
    (C) V
    (D) A

Darken Your Choice with HB Pencil

1.	(A) (B) (C) (D)	6.	(A) (B) (C) (D)	11.	(A) (B) (C) (D)	16	(A) (B) (C) (D)	21.	(A) (B) (C) (D)
2.	(A) (B) (C) (D)	7.	(A) (B) (C) (D)	12.	(A) (B) (C) (D)	17.	(A) (B) (C) (D)	22.	(A) (B) (C) (D)
3.	(A) (B) (C) (D)	8.	(A) (B) (C) (D)	13.	(A) (B) (C) (D)	18.	(A) (B) (C) (D)	23.	(A) (B) (C) (D)
4.	(A) (B) (C) (D)	9.	(A) (B) (C) (D)	14.	(A) (B) (C) (D)	19.	(A) (B) (C) (D)	24.	(A) (B) (C) (D)
5.	(A) (B) (C) (D)	10.	(A) (B) (C) (D)	15.	(A) (B) (C) (D)	20.	(A) (B) (C) (D)	25.	(A) (B) (C) (D)

VISUALIZING SOLID SHAPES

LEARNING OBJECTIVES

➤ Important formulas for different geometrical shapes

MULTIPLE CHOICE QUESTIONS

1. A boat having a length 3 m and breadth 2 m is floating on a lake. The boat sinks by 1 cm when a man gets on it. The mass of the man is:
   (A) 12 kg
   (B) 60 kg
   (C) 72 kg
   (D) 96 kg

2. 50 men took a dip in a water tank 40 m long and 20 m broad on a religious day. If the average displacement of water by a man is 4 m³, then the rise in the water level in the tank will be:
   (A) 20 cm
   (B) 25 cm
   (C) 35 cm
   (D) 50 cm

3. The slant height of a right circular cone is 10 m and its height is 8 m. Find the area of its curved surface.
   (A) 30π m²
   (B) 40π m²
   (C) 60π m²
   (D) 80π m²

4. A cistern 6m long and 4 m wide contains water up to a depth of 1 m 25 cm. The total area of wet surface is:
   (A) 49 m²
   (B) 50 m²
   (C) 53.5 m²
   (D) 55 m²

5. A metallic sheet is of rectangular shape with dimensions 48 m × 36 m. From each of its corners, a square is cut off so as to make an open box. If the length of the square is 8 m, the volume of the box (in m³) is:
   (A) 4830
   (B) 5120
   (C) 6420
   (D) 8960

6. The curved surface area of a cylindrical pillar is 264 m² and its volume is 924 m³. Find the ratio of its diameter to its height.

   (A) 3 : 7
   (B) 7 : 3
   (C) 6 : 7
   (D) 7 : 6

7. A cistern of capacity 8000 litres measures externally 3.3 m by 2.6 m by 1.1 m and its walls are 5 cm thick. The thickness of the base is:
   (A) 90 cm
   (B) 1 dm
   (C) 1 m
   (D) 1.1 cm

8. What is the total surface area of a right circular cone of height 14 cm and base radius 7 cm?
   (A) 344.35 cm²
   (B) 462 cm²
   (C) 498.35 cm²
   (D) None of these

9. A large cube is formed from the material obtained by melting three smaller cubes of sides 3, 4 and 5 cm. What is the ratio of the total surface areas of the smaller cubes and the large cube?
   (A) 2 : 1
   (B) 3 : 2
   (C) 25 : 18
   (D) 27 : 20

10. How many bricks, each measuring 25 cm × 11.25 cm × 6 cm, will be needed to build a wall of 8 m × 6 m × 22.5 cm?
    (A) 5600
    (B) 6000
    (C) 6400
    (D) 7200

11. What is the volume of a 32 metre high cylindrical tank?
    I. The area of its base is 154 m².
    II. The diameter of the base is 14 m.
    (A) I alone sufficient while II alone not sufficient to answer

(B) II alone sufficient while I alone not sufficient to answer

(C) Either I or II alone sufficient to answer

(D) Both I and II are not sufficient to answer

12. Is the given rectangular block a cube?
   I. At least 2 faces of the rectangular block are squares.
   II. The volume of the block is 64.
   (A) I alone sufficient while II alone not sufficient to answer
   (B) II alone sufficient while I alone not sufficient to answer
   (C) Either I or II alone sufficient to answer
   (D) Both I and II are not sufficient to answer

13. What is the capacity of this cylindrical tank?
   I. Radius of the base is half of its height which is 28 metres.
   II. Area of the base is 616 sq. metres and its height is 28 metres.
   (A) I alone sufficient while II alone not sufficient to answer
   (B) II alone sufficient while I alone not sufficient to answer
   (C) Either I or II alone sufficient to answer
   (D) Both I and II are not sufficient to answer

14. What is the height of this circular cone?
   I. The area of that cone is equal to the area of a rectangle whose length is 33 cm.
   II. The area of the base of that cone is 154 sq. cm.
   (A) I alone sufficient while II alone not sufficient to answer
   (B) II alone sufficient while I alone not sufficient to answer
   (C) Either I or II alone sufficient to answer
   (D) Both I and II are not sufficient to answer

15. What is the volume of a cube?
   I. The area of each face of the cube is 64 square metres.
   II. The length of one side of the cube is 8 metres.
   (A) I alone sufficient while II alone not sufficient to answer

16. What is the capacity of the cylindrical tank?
   I.   The area of the base is 61,600 sq. cm.
   II. The height of the tank is 1.5 times the radius.
   III. The circumference of base is 880 cm.
   (A) Only I and II
   (B) Only II and III
   (C) Only I and III
   (D) Only II and either I or III

17. Three pipes A, B and C can fill an empty tank fully in 30 minutes, 20 minutes, and 10 minutes respectively. When the tank is empty, all the three pipes are opened. A, B and C discharge chemical solutions P, Q and R respectively. What is the proportion of the solution R in the liquid in the tank after 3 minutes?
   (A) 5/11   (B) 6/11
   (C) 7/11   (D) 8/11

18. Pipes A and B can fill a tank in 5 and 6 hours respectively. Pipe C can empty it in 12 hours. If all the three pipes are opened together, then the tank will be filled in:
   (A) $1\frac{3}{17}$ hours   (B) $2\frac{8}{11}$ hours
   (C) $3\frac{9}{17}$ hours   (D) $4\frac{1}{2}$ hours

19. A pump can fill a tank with water in 2 hours. Because of a leak, it took $2\frac{1}{3}$ hours to fill the tank. The leak can drain all the water of the tank in:
   (A) 4 hours   (B) 7 hours
   (C) 8 hours   (D) 14 hours

20. Two pipes A and B can fill a cistern in 37.5 minutes and 45 minutes respectively. Both pipes are opened. The cistern will be filled in just half an hour, if B is turned off after:
   (A) 5 min.   (B) 9 min.
   (C) 10 min.   (D) 15 min.

21. Is the given rectangular block a cube?

    I. At least 2 faces of the rectangular block are squares.

    II. The volume of the block is 64.

    (A) I alone sufficient while II alone not sufficient to answer

    (B) II alone sufficient while I alone not sufficient to answer

    (C) Either I or II alone sufficient to answer

    (D) Both I and II are not sufficient to answer

22. What is the capacity of this cylindrical tank?

    I. Radius of the base is half of its height which is 28 metres.

    II. Area of the base is 616 sq. metres and its height is 28 metres.

    (A) I alone sufficient while II alone not sufficient to answer

    (B) II alone sufficient while I alone not sufficient to answer

    (C) Either I or II alone sufficient to answer

    (D) Both I and II are not sufficient to answer

23. How much time will the leak take to empty the full cistern?

    I. The cistern is normally filled in 9 hours.

    II. It takes one hour more than the usual time to fill the cistern because of a leak in the bottom.

    (A) I alone sufficient while II alone not sufficient to answer

    (B) II alone sufficient while I alone not sufficient to answer

    (C) Either I or II alone sufficient to answer

    (D) Both I and II are necessary to answer

24. How long will it take to empty the tank if both the inlet pipe A and the outlet pipe B are opened simultaneously?

    I. A can fill the tank in 16 minutes.

    II. B can empty the full tank in 8 minutes.

    (A) I alone sufficient while II alone not sufficient to answer

    (B) II alone sufficient while I alone not sufficient to answer

    (C) Either I or II alone sufficient to answer

    (D) Both I and II are necessary to answer

25. If both the pipes are opened, how many hours will be taken to fill the tank?

    I. The capacity of the tank is 400 litres.

    II. The pipe A fills the tank in 4 hours.

    III. The pipe B fills the tank in 6 hours.

    (A) Only I and II

    (B) Only II and III

    (C) All I, II and III

    (D) Any two of the three

1. Ⓐ Ⓑ Ⓒ Ⓓ	6. Ⓐ Ⓑ Ⓒ Ⓓ	11. Ⓐ Ⓑ Ⓒ Ⓓ	16 Ⓐ Ⓑ Ⓒ Ⓓ	21. Ⓐ Ⓑ Ⓒ Ⓓ
2. Ⓐ Ⓑ Ⓒ Ⓓ	7. Ⓐ Ⓑ Ⓒ Ⓓ	12. Ⓐ Ⓑ Ⓒ Ⓓ	17. Ⓐ Ⓑ Ⓒ Ⓓ	22. Ⓐ Ⓑ Ⓒ Ⓓ
3. Ⓐ Ⓑ Ⓒ Ⓓ	8. Ⓐ Ⓑ Ⓒ Ⓓ	13. Ⓐ Ⓑ Ⓒ Ⓓ	18. Ⓐ Ⓑ Ⓒ Ⓓ	23. Ⓐ Ⓑ Ⓒ Ⓓ
4. Ⓐ Ⓑ Ⓒ Ⓓ	9. Ⓐ Ⓑ Ⓒ Ⓓ	14. Ⓐ Ⓑ Ⓒ Ⓓ	19. Ⓐ Ⓑ Ⓒ Ⓓ	24. Ⓐ Ⓑ Ⓒ Ⓓ
5. Ⓐ Ⓑ Ⓒ Ⓓ	10. Ⓐ Ⓑ Ⓒ Ⓓ	15. Ⓐ Ⓑ Ⓒ Ⓓ	20. Ⓐ Ⓑ Ⓒ Ⓓ	25. Ⓐ Ⓑ Ⓒ Ⓓ

MATHEMATICAL REASONING 

16

LEARNING OBJECTIVES

➤ Solving questions related to mathematical reasoning

MULTIPLE CHOICE QUESTIONS

1. Ravi got twice as many sums wrong as he got correct. If he attempted 96 sums in all, how many sums did he solve correctly.
   (A) 16   (B) 32
   (C) 44   (D) 48

2. In the numbers from 1 to 100, how many times does 7 occur?
   (A) 17   (B) 18
   (C) 19   (D) 20

3. If 100 workers can finish a work in 100 days, then 40 workers can finish the work in how many days?
   (A) 40   (B) 120
   (C) 250   (D) 240

4. A group of students decided to go on a picnic and decided to spend ₹96 on eatables. Four of them did not turn up, after that the remaining students had to contribute extra ₹4 each. What was the number of students in the beginning?
   (A) 4   (B) 6
   (C) 8   (D) 12

5. A bus starts from city A. The number of women in the bus is half the number of men. In city B, 10 men leave the bus and 5 women enters. Now number of men and women is equal. What is the number of passengers in the beginning?
   (A) 35   (B) 45
   (C) 60   (D) 75

6. What is the least number of ducks that can swim in a way such that two ducks to front of a duck, two ducks behind a duck and a duck between two ducks?
   (A) 3   (B) 4
   (C) 5   (D) 6

7. If a clock takes seven seconds to strike seven, how long will it take to strike 10?
   (A) 10 seconds   (B) 9 seconds
   (C) $10\dfrac{1}{2}$ seconds   (D) None of these

8. The total of present ages of Mihir, Sonu and Ritesh is 86 years. What will be the total age of these three after 2 years?
   (A) 89 years
   (B) 91 years
   (C) 92 years
   (D) 94 years

9. In a caravan, in addition to 50 hens, there are 45 goats and 8 camels with some keepers. If the total number of feet is 224 more than the number of heads in the caravan, what is the number of keepers?
   (A) 5   (B) 10
   (C) 15   (D) 20

10. Out of 450 students, 270 students passed. What is the percentage of students who did not pass?

(A) 50% (B) 60%

(C) 40% (D) None of these

11. What will be the number which when added to itself 13 times, gives 112?

(A) 8 (B) 6

(C) 9 (D) 12

12. In a family, each daughter has the same number of brothers as she has sisters and each son has twice as many sisters as he has brothers. How many sons are there in the family?

(A) 1 (B) 2

(C) 3 (D) 4

13. The total of present ages of Ram, Shyam & Mohan is 96 years. What was the total of their ages three years ago?

(A) 93 years (B) 92 years

(C) 89 years (D) 87 years

14. Mr. Sharma is three times as old as his son. Five years back, he was four times as old as his son. What is the age of Mr. Sharma?

(A) 30 years (B) 45 years

(C) 48 years (D) 63 years

15. A train is moving at the speed of 72 km/hr In how many seconds will it cross an electric pole if the length of the train is 360m?

(A) 12 sec. (B) 15 sec.

(C) 18 sec. (D) 21 sec.

16. By selling an item at ₹. 720, Manish gains 20%. What is its cost price?

(A) 560 (B) 600

(C) 620 (D) 650

17. Manoj is twice as old as Monu. 3 years ago Manoj was three times as old as Monu. What is the present age of Manoj?

(A) 6 years

(B) 12 years

(C) 18 years

(D) 24 years

18. What is the product of all the numbers in the dial of a telephone?

(A) 158460

(B) 158480

(C) 159480

(D) None of these

19. At the end of a meeting, ten people present shake hands with each other once. What is the total number of handshakes?

(A) 45 (B) 55

(C) 60 (D) 65

Direction (20 to 25) : If + means ×, × means −, ÷ means + and '−' means ÷, then find the value in each of the following

20. $175 - 25 \div 5 + 20 \times 3 + 10 = ?$

(A) 75 (B) 76

(C) 77 (D) 78

21. $225 - 15 + 9 \times 15 \div 3 = ?$

(A) 123 (B) 255

(C) 120 (D) 155

22. $23 \div 107 \times 135 - 5 + 3 = ?$

(A) 47 (B) 49

(C) 59 (D) 57

23. $297 \times 57 \times 345 - 15 + 11 \div 18$

(A) 5 (B) 15

(C) 25 (D) 35

24. $78 - 13 + 7 \times 6 \div 17 + 3$

(A) 67 (B) 87

(C) 77 (D) 97

25. $123 \times 4 + 7 \div 76 - 19 + 7$

(A) 123 (B) 861

(C) 128 (D) None of these

26. Ravi got twice as many sums wrong as he got correct. If he attempted 96 sums in all, how many sums did he solve correctly.

    (A) 16   (B) 32
    (C) 44   (D) 48

27. If 100 workers can finish a work in 100 days, then 40 workers can finish the work in how many days?

    (A) 40   (B) 120
    (C) 250   (D) 240

28. A group of students decided to go on a picnic and decided to spend ₹96 on eatables. Four of them did not turn up, after that the remaining ones had to contribute ₹4 each extra. What was the number of students in the beginning?

    (A) 4   (B) 6
    (C) 8   (D) 12

29. A bus starts from city A. The number of women in the bus is half the number of men. In city B, 10 men leave the bus and 5 women enters. Now number of men and women is equal. What is the number of passengers in the beginning?

    (A) 35
    (B) 45
    (C) 60
    (D) 75

30. What is the least number of ducks that can swim in a way such that two ducks to front of a duck, two ducks behind a duck and a duck between two ducks?

    (A) 3
    (B) 4
    (C) 5
    (D) 6

—Darken Your Choice with HB Pencil—

1.	Ⓐ Ⓑ Ⓒ Ⓓ	7.	Ⓐ Ⓑ Ⓒ Ⓓ	13.	Ⓐ Ⓑ Ⓒ Ⓓ	19	Ⓐ Ⓑ Ⓒ Ⓓ	25.	Ⓐ Ⓑ Ⓒ Ⓓ
2.	Ⓐ Ⓑ Ⓒ Ⓓ	8.	Ⓐ Ⓑ Ⓒ Ⓓ	14.	Ⓐ Ⓑ Ⓒ Ⓓ	20.	Ⓐ Ⓑ Ⓒ Ⓓ	26.	Ⓐ Ⓑ Ⓒ Ⓓ
3.	Ⓐ Ⓑ Ⓒ Ⓓ	9.	Ⓐ Ⓑ Ⓒ Ⓓ	15.	Ⓐ Ⓑ Ⓒ Ⓓ	21.	Ⓐ Ⓑ Ⓒ Ⓓ	27.	Ⓐ Ⓑ Ⓒ Ⓓ
4.	Ⓐ Ⓑ Ⓒ Ⓓ	10.	Ⓐ Ⓑ Ⓒ Ⓓ	16.	Ⓐ Ⓑ Ⓒ Ⓓ	22.	Ⓐ Ⓑ Ⓒ Ⓓ	28.	Ⓐ Ⓑ Ⓒ Ⓓ
5.	Ⓐ Ⓑ Ⓒ Ⓓ	11.	Ⓐ Ⓑ Ⓒ Ⓓ	17.	Ⓐ Ⓑ Ⓒ Ⓓ	23.	Ⓐ Ⓑ Ⓒ Ⓓ	29.	Ⓐ Ⓑ Ⓒ Ⓓ
6.	Ⓐ Ⓑ Ⓒ Ⓓ	12.	Ⓐ Ⓑ Ⓒ Ⓓ	18.	Ⓐ Ⓑ Ⓒ Ⓓ	24.	Ⓐ Ⓑ Ⓒ Ⓓ	30.	Ⓐ Ⓑ Ⓒ Ⓓ

LOGICAL REASONING

17

LEARNING OBJECTIVES

- ➤ Solving questions related to patterns
- ➤ Solving questions related to number series
- ➤ Solving questions related to alphabetical series
- ➤ Solving questions related to odd one out concept
- ➤ Concept of Coding and Decoding
- ➤ Letter word problems
- ➤ Alphabet Quibbl

- ➤ Solving questions related to patterns
- ➤ Solving questions related to direction sense test
- ➤ Number test
- ➤ Embedded Figures
- ➤ Solving figure based questions related to odd one out
- ➤ Solving questions related to Dice pattern

MULTIPLE CHOICE QUESTIONS

1.

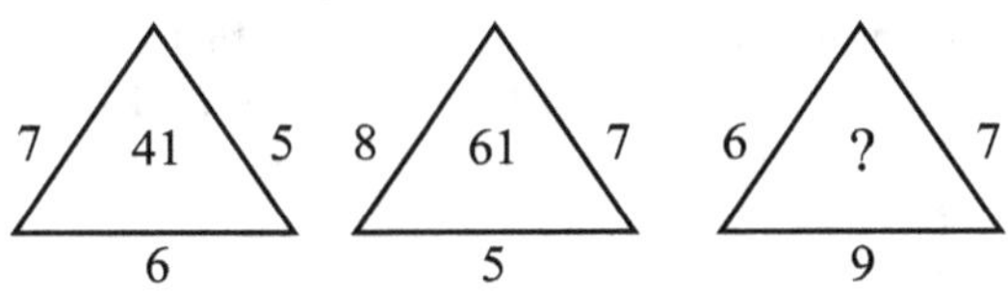

(A) 61
(B) 71
(C) 51
(D) 59

2.

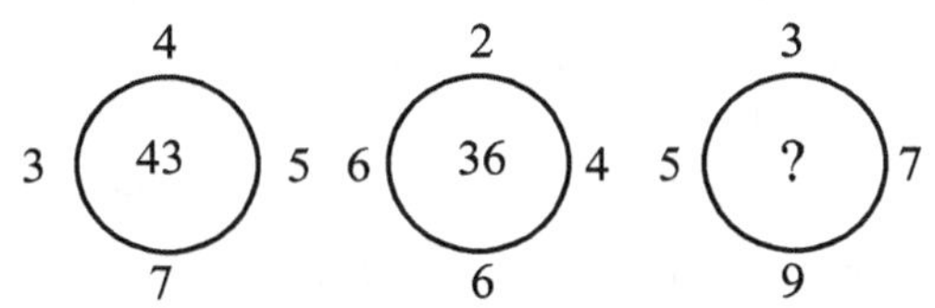

(A) 62   (B) 52
(C) 72   (D) 82

3.

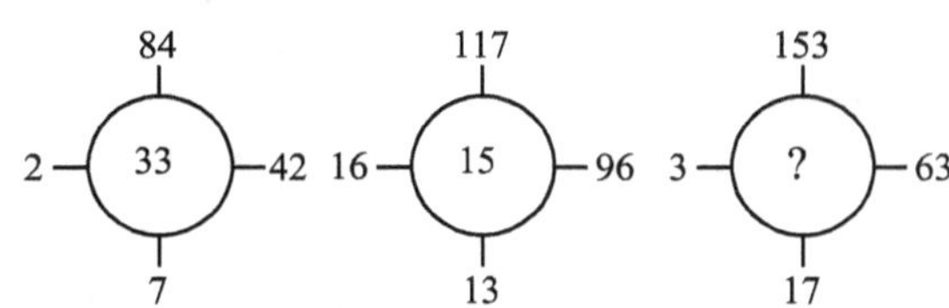

(A) 28   (B) 30
(C) 31   (D) 32

4. 1000, 200, 40, __
(A) 8   (B) 10
(C) 15   (D) 20

5. 5.2, 4.8, 4.4, 4, __
(A) 3   (B) 3.3
(C) 3.5   (D) 3.6

6. 2, 6, 18, 54, __
(A) 108   (B) 148
(C) 162   (D) 216

7. _ op _ mo _ n _ _ pnmop _.
   (A) mnpmon   (B) mpnmop
   (C) mnompn   (D) mnpomn

8. _ bcc _ ac _ aabb _ ab _ cc
   (A) aabca   (B) abaca
   (C) bacab   (D) bcaca

9. m _ nm _ n _ an _ a _ ma _
   (A) aamnan   (B) ammanm
   (C) aammnn   (D) amammn

10. 3, 5, 7, 12, 17, 19
   (A) 19   (B) 17
   (C) 5   (D) 12

11. 41, 43, 47, 53, 61, 71, 73, 81
   (A) 61   (B) 71
   (C) 73   (D) 81

12. 835, 734, 642, 751, 853, 981, 532
   (A) 751   (B) 853
   (C) 981   (D) 532

13. In a certain language, SIGHT is written as FVTUC, how is REVEAL written in the same language?
   (A) ERIRNY   (B) DQHQMX
   (C) FSJSOZ   (D) YNRIRE

14. If in a certain language, MADRAS is coded as NBESBT, how is BOMBAY coded in that language?
   (A) CPNCBZ   (B) CPNCBX
   (C) CPOCBZ   (D) CQOCBZ

15. In a certain code, ROAD is written as URDG, how is SWAN written in that code?
   (A) VZCP   (B) UXDQ
   (C) VZDQ   (D) VXDQ

16.
   (A) Waving   (B) Watching
   (C) Waiting   (D) Wanting

17.
   (a) Lapse   (b) Leave
   (c) Leisure   (d) Laurel

18.
   (A) Protein   (B) Proverb
   (C) Property   (D) Project

19. Pointing to a man on the stage, Ritu said, "He is the brother of the daughter of the wife of my husband." How is the man on the stage related to Ritu?
   (A) Husband   (B) Cousin
   (C) Nephew   (D) Son

20. A party consists of grandmother, father, mother, four sons and their wives and one son and two daughters to each of the sons. How many females are there in all?
   (A) 14   (B) 19
   (C) 12   (D) 25

21. Lata and Mona are Ravi's wives. Shalu is Mona's Step-daughter. How is Lata related to Shalu?
   (A) Sister   (B) Mother-in-Law
   (C) Mother   (D) Step-mother

22. From his house, Lokesh went 15 km to the North. Then he turned toward West and covered 10 km. Then he turned towards South and covered 5 km. Finally turning to the East, he covered 10 km. In which direction is he from his house?
   (A) East   (B) West
   (C) North   (D) South

23. Sachin walks 20 km towards North. He turns left and walks 40 km. He again turns left and walks 20 km. Finally he moves 20 km after turning to the left. How far is he from his starting position?
   (A) 20 km   (B) 30 km
   (C) 50 km   (D) 60 km

24. Sundar runs 20 m towards East and turns to right and runs 10 m. Then he turns to the right and runs 9 m. Again he turns to right and runs 5 m. After this he turns to left and runs 12 m and finally he turns to right and moves 6 m. Now to which direction is Sundar facing?
   (A) East   (B) West
   (C) North   (D) South

25. How many 7s are preceded by 9 and followed by 6?
   (A) 1   (B) 2
   (C) 3   (D) 4

26. Which digits have equal frequency?
   (A) 2, 5, 8   (B) 2, 5, 6
   (C) 4, 5, 9   (D) 3, 4, 9

27. Which digit has highest frequency?
   (A) 5   (B) 6
   (C) 7   (D) 9

28. Choose the figure which is different from the rest.

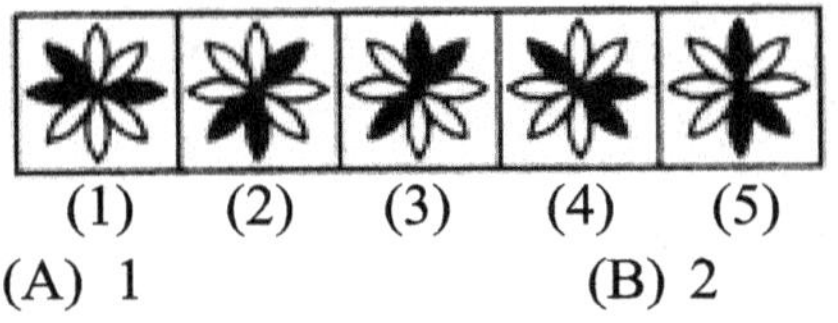

   (1)   (2)   (3)   (4)   (5)
   (A) 1   (B) 2
   (C) 3   (D) 4
   (E) 5

29. Choose the figure which is different from the rest.

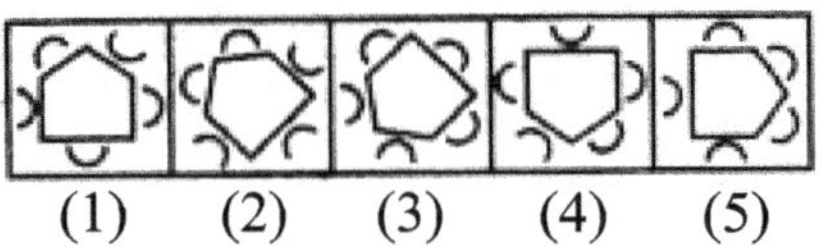

   (1)   (2)   (3)   (4)   (5)
   (A) 1   (B) 2
   (C) 3   (D) 4
   (E) 5

30. Choose the figure which is different from the rest.

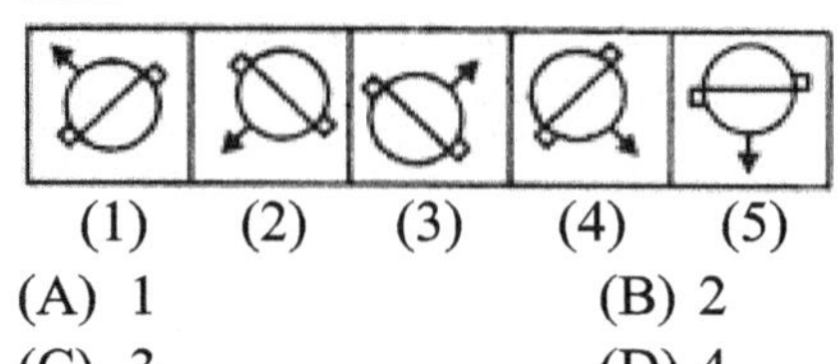

   (1)   (2)   (3)   (4)   (5)
   (A) 1   (B) 2
   (C) 3   (D) 4
   (E) 5

1.	Ⓐ Ⓑ Ⓒ Ⓓ	7.	Ⓐ Ⓑ Ⓒ Ⓓ	13.	Ⓐ Ⓑ Ⓒ Ⓓ	19	Ⓐ Ⓑ Ⓒ Ⓓ	25.	Ⓐ Ⓑ Ⓒ Ⓓ
2.	Ⓐ Ⓑ Ⓒ Ⓓ	8.	Ⓐ Ⓑ Ⓒ Ⓓ	14.	Ⓐ Ⓑ Ⓒ Ⓓ	20.	Ⓐ Ⓑ Ⓒ Ⓓ	26.	Ⓐ Ⓑ Ⓒ Ⓓ
3.	Ⓐ Ⓑ Ⓒ Ⓓ	9.	Ⓐ Ⓑ Ⓒ Ⓓ	15.	Ⓐ Ⓑ Ⓒ Ⓓ	21.	Ⓐ Ⓑ Ⓒ Ⓓ	27.	Ⓐ Ⓑ Ⓒ Ⓓ
4.	Ⓐ Ⓑ Ⓒ Ⓓ	10.	Ⓐ Ⓑ Ⓒ Ⓓ	16.	Ⓐ Ⓑ Ⓒ Ⓓ	22.	Ⓐ Ⓑ Ⓒ Ⓓ	28.	Ⓐ Ⓑ Ⓒ Ⓓ
5.	Ⓐ Ⓑ Ⓒ Ⓓ	11.	Ⓐ Ⓑ Ⓒ Ⓓ	17.	Ⓐ Ⓑ Ⓒ Ⓓ	23.	Ⓐ Ⓑ Ⓒ Ⓓ	29.	Ⓐ Ⓑ Ⓒ Ⓓ
6.	Ⓐ Ⓑ Ⓒ Ⓓ	12.	Ⓐ Ⓑ Ⓒ Ⓓ	18.	Ⓐ Ⓑ Ⓒ Ⓓ	24.	Ⓐ Ⓑ Ⓒ Ⓓ	30.	Ⓐ Ⓑ Ⓒ Ⓓ

MODEL TEST PAPER

MULTIPLE CHOICE QUESTIONS

1. Sum of two integers is 32. If one of the integer is −32, then the other is:
   - (a) 64
   - (b) 32
   - (c) −32
   - (d) −64

2. The smallest possible decimal fraction upto three decimal places is:
   - (a) 0.001
   - (b) 0.011
   - (c) 0.101
   - (d) 0.111

3. Find the value of the expression given by $(2/3)^2 \times (3/4)^2 \times (4/9)^0$.
   - (a) 116
   - (b) 14
   - (c) 18
   - (d) 29

4. Find the value of $a^2 + b^2 + c^2 - ab - bc - ca$, if $a = 1$, $b = 2$ and $c = 3$.
   - (a) 2
   - (b) 1
   - (c) 3
   - (d) 7

5. The ratio of 700 g to 6 kg is:
   - (a) 7 : 6
   - (b) 7 : 60
   - (c) 6 : 13
   - (d) 6 : 11

6. 1/2 is what percent of 1/3 ?
   - (a) 4 %
   - (b) 150 %
   - (c) 2 %
   - (d) 1200 %

7. If selling price of 10 note books is same as cost price of 5 note books then find the loss %.
   - (a) 20%
   - (b) 30%
   - (c) 40%
   - (d) 50%

8. Find the simple interest on Rs. 5, 000 for 2 years at 8 % per annum.
   - (a) Rs. 800
   - (b) Rs. 900
   - (c) Rs. 850
   - (d) Rs. 875

9. Find the area of rectangle, whose length is 1.5 m and breadth is 30 cm.
   - (a) 45 cm²
   - (b) 450 cm²
   - (c) 4500 cm²
   - (d) 455 cm²

10. At a particular place temperature of the weekdays is shown in the table given below. Find the difference between highest and the lowest temperature.

Day	Temperature °C
Monday	−20°C
Tuesday	−5°C
Wednesday	15°C
Thursday	10°C
Friday	−15°C
Saturday	−12°C
Sunday	14°C

   - (a) 35°C
   - (b) −25°C
   - (c) −35°C
   - (d) 20°C

11. Order the following rational numbers from least to greatest. −4, 6, 9, 0, −19, −8, 8, 2,
   - (a) 0, 2, 4, −4, 6, 8, −8, −19
   - (b) −4, −8, −19, 0, 2, 4, 6, 8
   - (c) −19, −8, −4, 0, 2, 6, 8, 9
   - (d) −19, −8, −4, 0, 4, 6, 8, 9

12. Simplify : $(a + b - c)^2 + (a - b - c)^2$
   - (a) $a^2 + b2 + c^2 - 2ca$
   - (b) $2a^2 + b2 + c^2 - 2ca$
   - (c) $2(a^2 + b2 + c^2 - 2ca)$
   - (d) $2(a^2 - b^2 + c^2 - 2ca)$

13. If $x : 8 :: 3 : 2$ then the value of x is :
   - (a) 14
   - (b) 12
   - (c) 15
   - (d) 10

14. In an examination, 96 % of the candidates passed and 100 failed. How many candidates appeared?
   - (a) 2500
   - (b) 2700
   - (c) 2750
   - (d) 2900

OLYMPIAD WORKBOOK (IMO) CLASS – 7

15. A bicycle was purchased for Rs. 1800 and sold for Rs. 2000. Find the gain percent.
    (a) 13%
    (b) 11.11%
    (c) 15%
    (d) 18%

16. From the following table find the values of p, q and r.

Scores	Tally Mark	Frequency
0	II	r
1	I	1
25	I	1
34	p	3
67	II	2
71	I	q
73	I	1

    (a) $p \to$ III, $q = 2$ and $r = 2$
    (b) $p \to$ III, $q = 1$ and $r = 1$
    (c) $p \to$ II, $q = 1$ and $r = 2$
    (d) $p \to$ III, $q = 1$ and $r = 2$

17. The diagrammatic representation with the help of pictures is called:
    (a) Cartogram
    (b) Pie chart
    (c) Pictogram
    (d) Bar chart

18. Which of the following cannot be the sides of a right angled triangle?
    (a) 3 cm, 4 cm and 5 cm
    (b) 6 cm, 8 cm and 10 cm
    (c) 6 cm, 9 cm and 12 cm
    (d) 5 cm, 12 cm and 13 cm

19. Which one of the following is equal to $25x^2 + 4y^2 + 20xy$?
    (a) $(5x + 2y)^2$
    (b) $(5x - 2y)^2$
    (c) $(x + 2y)^2$
    (d) $(9x + 3y)^2$

20. Find the supplement of an angle which is 5 times of its complement.
    (a) $150°$
    (b) $105°$
    (c) $130°$
    (d) $60°$

21. If $4A = 5B$ and $6B = 7C$, then $A : C$ is equal to:
    (a) $35 : 24$
    (b) $8 : 9$
    (c) $24 : 35$
    (d) $14 : 15$

22. The marked price of an article is Rs. 540 and the shopkeeper allows a successive discount of 15% and 20% on it. Find the selling price of the article.
    (a) Rs. 367.20
    (b) Rs. 351.00
    (c) Rs. 351.20
    (d) Rs. 351.67

23. Which shall come next in the series given below?
    6, 12, 20, 30, ?
    (a) 40
    (b) 42
    (c) 52
    (d) 48

24. Find the mean proportional between 16 and 81.
    (a) 24
    (b) 32
    (c) 36
    (d) 42

25. Taking today as zero on the number line if the day before yesterday is 24 February 2016, what is the day, 6 days after tomorrow?
    (a) Thursday
    (b) Friday
    (c) Saturday
    (d) Wednesday

26. Find the value of $4xy(x - y) - 6x^2(y - y^2) - 3y^2(2x^2 - x) + 2xy(x - y)$ for $x = 5$ and $y = 13$.
    (a) -1955
    (b) 2535
    (c) -2535
    (d) 1955

27. The denominator of a rational number is greater than its numerator by 6. If the numerator is increased by 5 and the denominator is decreased by 3 then the number obtained is 5/4. Find the rational number.
    (a) 5/11
    (b) 13/19
    (c) 11/17
    (d) 7/13

28. A sum of money doubles itself in 10 years at simple interest. In how many years would it triple itself?
    (a) 10
    (b) 15
    (c) 20
    (d) 25

29. What is the total number of candidates who appeared in an examination, if 31% has failed and the number of passed candidates are 247 more than the number of failed candidates?
    (a) 650
    (b) 750
    (c) 800
    (d) 900

30. The price of pure mustard oil is Rs. 100 per litre. A shopkeeper adulterates it with some other types of oils at Rs. 50 per litre. He sells the mixture at the rate of Rs. 96 per litreso as to gain 20 % on the whole transaction. The ratio in which he mixed the two oils is:
(a) 1 : 2   (b) 2 : 3
(c) 3 : 2   (d) 1 : 4

31. If the simple interest on a certain sum for 3 years at the rate of 8% per annum is half of the compound interest on Rs. 4000 for 2 years at the rate of 10% per annum, then the sum for simple interest is:
(a) Rs. 1230   (b) Rs. 1250
(c) Rs. 1730   (d) Rs. 1750

32. Veer performs his project work on a number of students who like soft drinks of different flavors in a school. After collecting the data he wants to know the most flavored soft drink which is liked by most of the students. Which central tendency makes his wish true?
(a) Mean   (b) Row data
(c) Median   (d) Mode

33. The first, second and third class fares between New Delhi and Chandigarh were in the ratio 10 : 8 : 3 and the number of the first, second and third class passengers between the two stations was in the ratio 3 : 4 : 10. If the total sales of tickets is Rs. 161000 per day, find the money obtained by the sales of second class tickets.
(a) Rs. 58000   (b) Rs. 56000
(c) Rs. 48700   (d) Rs. 32200

34. The interior angle of a regular polygon exceeds its exterior angle by 108°. The number of sides of the polygon is
(a) 14   (b) 12
(c) 10   (d) 16

35. The variable x varies directly as y and varies inversely as z. When $x = 8$, $y = 12$, then $z = 3$. What is x when $z = 6$ and $y = 24$?
(a) 2   (b) 4
(c) 8   (d) 12

36. Two blends of a commodity costing Rs. 35 and Rs. 40 kg respectively are mixed in the ratio 2 : 3 by weight. If one-fifth of the mixture is sold at Rs. 46 per kg and the remaining at the rate of Rs. 55 per kg, then the profit percent is
(a) 20   (b) 30
(c) 40   (d) 50

37. A and B can do a given piece of work in 8 days, B and C can do the same work in 12 days and A, B, C can complete it in 6 days. The number of days required to finish the work by A and C is
(a) 16   (b) 12
(c) 8   (d) 24

38. Height of a certain flag pole is 60 feet. Grease is applied to the pole. A monkey attempts to climb the pole. It climbs 5 feet every second but slips down 2ft the next second. When will the monkey reach the top of the flag pole?
(a) 48 seconds   (b) 39 seconds
(c) 30 seconds   (d) 29 seconds

39. Anita and Geeta are experts in dance and music. Seeta and Geeta are experts in music and painting. Anita and Neeta are experts in debate and dance. Neeta and Seeta are experts in painting and debate. Who is/are not expert in painting?
(a) Anita only   (b) Seeta only
(c) Anita and Geeta   (d) Neeta only

40. Replace the question mark with the correct number.

15	225	30
7	70	20
3	?	8

(a) 12   (b) 16
(c) 24   (d) 70

41. If 'MANGO' is coded as 50 and 'ORANGE' is coded as 60, then what is the code for PINEAPPLE'?
(a) 84   (b) 85
(c) 90   (d) 94

42. Find the missing term in the following sequence. ACH, FAI, JYK, MWN, ______ .
(a) PVS   (b) OUR
(c) PTQ   (d) OTS

43. Six members of a family A, B, C, D, E and F are travelling together. B is the son of C but C is not the mother of B. A and C are a married couple. E is the brother of C. D is the daughter of A. F is the brother of B. How many male members are there in the family?

(a) 1   (b) 2

(c) 3   (d) 4

44. Select the set of letters missing in the following series. bdabcdbdabcd_dabcdb_abcdbd_

(a) bcd   (b) bda

(c) dbc   (d) cda

45. Choose the item which is not similar to the other items.

(a) 8, 24   (b) 7, 22

(c) 5, 16   (d) 14, 43

46. Find the wrong number in the given series. 142, 119, 100, 83, 65, 59, 52

(a) 119   (b) 100

(c) 83   (d) 65

47. Mr. Prakash and Mr. Prem each bought the same motorcycle using a 10% off coupon. Mr. Prakash's cashier took 10% off the price and then added 8.5% sales tax whereas Mr. Prem's cashier first added the sales tax and then took 10% off the total price. The amount Mr. Prakash paid is

(a) same as the amount Mr. Prem paid.

(b) greater by Rs. 850 from the amount Mr. Prem paid.

(c) lesser by Rs. 550 from the amount Mr. Prem paid.

(d) greater by Rs. 85 from the amount Mr. Prem paid.

48. Three glasses of equal volume contains acid mixed with water. The ratios of acid and water in the three glasses are $2 : 3$, $3 : 4$ and $4 : 5$ respectively. The contents of these glasses are poured in a larger vessel. The ratio of acid and water in the large vessel is

(a) 407 : 560   (b) 411 : 564

(c) 417 : 564   (d) 401 : 544

49. If $x + y = 6$ and $x^3 + y^3 = 72$, then the value of xy is:

(a) 12   (b) 8

(c) 6   (d) 9

50. The area of the parallelogram whose length is 30 cm, width is 20 cm and one diagonal is 40 cm, is

(a) $100\sqrt{15}$ cm^2 (b) $150\sqrt{15}$ cm^2

(c) $200\sqrt{15}$ cm^2 (d) $300\sqrt{15}$ cm^2

Darken Your Choice with HB Pencil

1.	Ⓐ Ⓑ Ⓒ Ⓓ	11.	Ⓐ Ⓑ Ⓒ Ⓓ	21.	Ⓐ Ⓑ Ⓒ Ⓓ	31.	Ⓐ Ⓑ Ⓒ Ⓓ	41.	Ⓐ Ⓑ Ⓒ Ⓓ
2.	Ⓐ Ⓑ Ⓒ Ⓓ	12.	Ⓐ Ⓑ Ⓒ Ⓓ	22	Ⓐ Ⓑ Ⓒ Ⓓ	32.	Ⓐ Ⓑ Ⓒ Ⓓ	42.	Ⓐ Ⓑ Ⓒ Ⓓ
3.	Ⓐ Ⓑ Ⓒ Ⓓ	13.	Ⓐ Ⓑ Ⓒ Ⓓ	23.	Ⓐ Ⓑ Ⓒ Ⓓ	33.	Ⓐ Ⓑ Ⓒ Ⓓ	43.	Ⓐ Ⓑ Ⓒ Ⓓ
4.	Ⓐ Ⓑ Ⓒ Ⓓ	14.	Ⓐ Ⓑ Ⓒ Ⓓ	24.	Ⓐ Ⓑ Ⓒ Ⓓ	34.	Ⓐ Ⓑ Ⓒ Ⓓ	44.	Ⓐ Ⓑ Ⓒ Ⓓ
5.	Ⓐ Ⓑ Ⓒ Ⓓ	15.	Ⓐ Ⓑ Ⓒ Ⓓ	25.	Ⓐ Ⓑ Ⓒ Ⓓ	35.	Ⓐ Ⓑ Ⓒ Ⓓ	45.	Ⓐ Ⓑ Ⓒ Ⓓ
6.	Ⓐ Ⓑ Ⓒ Ⓓ	16.	Ⓐ Ⓑ Ⓒ Ⓓ	26.	Ⓐ Ⓑ Ⓒ Ⓓ	36.	Ⓐ Ⓑ Ⓒ Ⓓ	46.	Ⓐ Ⓑ Ⓒ Ⓓ
7.	Ⓐ Ⓑ Ⓒ Ⓓ	17.	Ⓐ Ⓑ Ⓒ Ⓓ	27.	Ⓐ Ⓑ Ⓒ Ⓓ	37.	Ⓐ Ⓑ Ⓒ Ⓓ	47.	Ⓐ Ⓑ Ⓒ Ⓓ
8.	Ⓐ Ⓑ Ⓒ Ⓓ	18.	Ⓐ Ⓑ Ⓒ Ⓓ	28.	Ⓐ Ⓑ Ⓒ Ⓓ	38.	Ⓐ Ⓑ Ⓒ Ⓓ	48.	Ⓐ Ⓑ Ⓒ Ⓓ
9.	Ⓐ Ⓑ Ⓒ Ⓓ	19.	Ⓐ Ⓑ Ⓒ Ⓓ	29.	Ⓐ Ⓑ Ⓒ Ⓓ	39.	Ⓐ Ⓑ Ⓒ Ⓓ	49.	Ⓐ Ⓑ Ⓒ Ⓓ
10.	Ⓐ Ⓑ Ⓒ Ⓓ	20.	Ⓐ Ⓑ Ⓒ Ⓓ	30.	Ⓐ Ⓑ Ⓒ Ⓓ	40.	Ⓐ Ⓑ Ⓒ Ⓓ	50.	Ⓐ Ⓑ Ⓒ Ⓓ

HINTS AND SOLUTIONS

1. INTEGERS

Answer Key

1. (A)	2. (B)	3. (C)	4. (B)	5. (C)	6. (A)	7. (B)	8. (D)	9. (D)	10. (A)
11. (C)	12. (B)	13. (C)	14. (B)	15. (D)	16. (A)	17. (A)	18. (B)	19. (A)	20. (B)

1. **(A)**
   p is the successor of q
   $\Rightarrow p = q + 1$
   $\therefore q - p - 4 = q - (q + 1) - 4$
   $= q - q - 1 - 4$
   $= -5$

2. **(B)**
   $63 - 98 - (-58) + 115 + (-172) + 78 + (-62) + 131$
   $= 63 - 98 + 58 + 115 - 172 + 78 - 62 + 131$
   $= 445 - 332$
   $= 113$

3. **(C)**
   Profit earned by selling 45 copies = ₹45
   Total loss = ₹5
   Profit earned + loss incurred = Total loss.
   $\Rightarrow 45 + $ Loss incurred $= -5$
   $\Rightarrow$ Loss incurred $= -5 - 45 = -50$
   $\qquad\qquad\qquad = -5000$ Paise
   Number of Pens sold $= \dfrac{5000}{4} = 125$

4. **(B)**
   By definition

5. **(C)**
   $8°C - 11°C = -3°C$

6. **(A)**
   Profit by selling white cement $= 8 \times 3000$
   $\qquad\qquad\qquad\qquad\quad = 24000$
   Loss by selling grey cement $= 5 \times 5000$
   $\qquad\qquad\qquad\qquad\quad = 25000$

Loss $= 25000 - 24000 = 1000$

7. **(B)**
   Fundamental property

8. **(D)**
   $10°C + x = -8°C$
   $\Rightarrow x = [-8°C] + [-10°C]$
   $\Rightarrow x = -18°C$
   No. of hours $= \dfrac{-18°C}{-2°C} = 9$
   9 hours from 12 noon is 9 P.M.

9. **(D)**
   Decrease in price $= ₹35 \times 7 = ₹245$
   New price $= ₹500 - ₹245 = ₹255$

10. **(A)**
    Descend after 7 hours $= 500 \times 7 = 3500$m
    Height at which hikers are on the mountain
    after 7 hrs $= 6048 - 3500 = 2548$m

11. **(C)**
    Total distance $= 14$m $+ 250$m $= 264$m
    Time taken $= \dfrac{264\text{m}}{4\text{m / min}} = 66$ min

12. **(B)**
    $888 - 777 + 555$
    $= 111 \times 8 - 111 \times 7 + 111 \times 5$
    $= 111 \times (8 - 7 + 5) = 111 \times 6$

13. **(C)**
    $14 - \{12 - \{9 - (7 - 6 - 2)\}\}]$
    $= [14 - \{12 - \{9 - (7 - 4)\}\}]$
    $= [14 - \{12 - \{9 - 3\}\}]$
    $= [14 - \{12 - 6\}]$

OLYMPIAD WORKBOOK (IMO) CLASS – 7

$= 14 - 6 = 8$

14. (B)

Let the floor be *x, then*

$x + 13 - 5 + 6 - 8 = 7$

$\Rightarrow x + 6 = 7$

$\Rightarrow x = 7 - 6 = 1$

She started from 1st floor.

15. (D)

Fundamental property

16. (A)

Ascending order: $-7, -4, -2, \boxed{-1}, 1, 3, 9$

17. (A)

A is 5 and B is -7. so option (a) is not true.

18. (B)

P is -5, Q is 0, R is 5, S is 10.

19. (A)

is 5, @ is 2, $ is -1 and & is -5,

so the ascending order is &$@#.

20. (B)

$32° - 23° = 9°$

$1° - (-10°) = 11°$

$-11° - (-18°) = 7°$

$5° - (-5°) = 10°$

HOTS (ACHIEVERS SECTION)

21. (D)	22. (B)	23. (C)	24. (B)	25. (D)

2. FRACTIONS AND DECIMALS

Answer Key

1. (A)	2. (D)	3. (C)	4. (B)	5. (C)	6. (D)	7. (A)	8. (C)	9. (D)	10. (A)
11. (C)	12. (B)	13. (C)	14. (C)	15. (C)	16. (D)	17. (A)	18. (D)	19. (A)	20. (A)

1. (A)

From A to J there are 10 letters.

So, letter at $\frac{2}{5}$ place $= \left(\frac{2}{5} \times 10\right)$th letter = 4th

letter = D

2. (D)

Let the number be x.

According to the question, $\frac{2}{3}$ of x = 10

$\Rightarrow \frac{2}{3} \times x = 10$

On multiplying both sides by $\frac{3}{2}$ we get

$\frac{2}{3} \times x \times \frac{3}{2} = 10 \times \frac{3}{2} \Rightarrow x = 5 \times 3 \Rightarrow x = 15$

1.75 times of 15 = 1.75 of 15 = 1.75 × 15 =

$\frac{175}{100} \times 15 - \frac{2625}{100} - 26.25$

3. (C)

total number of students = 40   [given]

Students who eat rice only $= \frac{1}{5}$ of total students

$= \frac{1}{5} \times 40 = 8$

Student who eat chapati only $= \frac{2}{5} \times 40 = 16$

∴ Students who eat chapati and rice =

= Total number of students − (Students who eat rice only + Students who eat chapati only)

$= 40 - (8 + 16)$

$= 40 - 24 = 16$

∴ Fraction of students who eat both chapati and rice

$= \dfrac{\text{Number of students eat both chapati and rice}}{\text{Total number of students}}$

$= \frac{16}{40} = \frac{2}{5}$

4. (B)

Let total pages of the book be x.

According to the question, $\frac{1}{3}x + 40 = \frac{7}{10}x$

$40 = \frac{7}{10}x - \frac{1}{3}x = \frac{7x - 2x}{10}$

$40 = \frac{5x}{10}$

$x = \frac{400}{5} = 80$

$\therefore$ Total pages of the book = 80

Hence, pages left to be read = Total pages of

a book $-\left(\frac{7}{10}x\right)$

$= 80 - \frac{7}{10} \times 80$

$= 80 - 56 = 24$ pages

5. **(C)**

Given, $7\frac{1}{6} \div 3\frac{2}{3} = \frac{(7 \times 6) + 1}{6} \div \frac{(3 \times 3) + 2}{3}$

$= \frac{42 + 1}{6} \div \frac{9 + 2}{3} = \frac{43}{6} \div \frac{11}{3} = \frac{43}{6} \times \frac{3}{11}$

$= \frac{43}{22} = 1.95$

Obviously, $1.95 > 1.5$

Hence, $7\frac{1}{6} \div 3\frac{2}{3} > 1.5$

6. **(D)**

Given, $\dfrac{2\frac{1}{2} + \frac{1}{5}}{2\frac{1}{2} \div \frac{1}{5}} = \dfrac{\frac{(2 \times 2) + 1}{2} + \frac{1}{5}}{\frac{(2 \times 2) + 1}{2} \div \frac{1}{5}}$

$= \dfrac{\frac{5}{2} + \frac{1}{5}}{\frac{5}{2} \div \frac{1}{5}} = \dfrac{\frac{25 + 2}{10}}{\frac{5}{2} \times 5}$

$= \frac{27}{10} \div \frac{25}{2} = \frac{27}{10} \times \frac{2}{25} = \frac{27}{125}$

7. **(A)**

Given, normal body temperature = 98.6°F

and temperature rose to = 103.1°F

$\therefore$ Rise in temperature $(103.1°F - 98.6)°F = 4.5°F$

8. **(C)**

Let the number be x.

According to the question, $\frac{x}{520} = \frac{85}{0.625}$

$\Rightarrow x = \frac{85 \times 520 \times 1000}{625}$

$= \frac{44200000}{625}$ [by cross-multiplication]

$\Rightarrow x = 70720$

Hence, the number is 70720.

9. **(D)**

Cloth required in making one shirt

$= \left(2\frac{1}{4} + \frac{1}{8}\right) = \frac{(2 \times 4) + 1}{4} + \frac{1}{8}$

$= \frac{9}{4} + \frac{1}{8} = \frac{18 + 1}{8} = \frac{19}{8}$ m

$\therefore$ Total cloth required in making 6 such shirts = 6 × Cloth required in one shirt

$= 6 \times \frac{19}{8} = \frac{114}{8} = \frac{57}{4} = 14\frac{1}{4}$ m

Hence, $14\frac{1}{4}$ m cloth will be used in making. 6 shirts.

10. **(A)**

Given, picture hall has seats = 820

One usher guessed, picture hall was $\frac{3}{4}$ full.

$\therefore \frac{3}{4}$ of $820 = \frac{3}{4} \times 820 = \frac{3 \times 820}{4} = \frac{2460}{4} = 615$

Another usher guessed, picture hall was $\frac{2}{3}$ full.

$\therefore \frac{2}{3}$ of $820 = \frac{2}{3} \times 820 = \frac{2 \times 820}{3} = \frac{1640}{3} = 546.66$

Since, 648 tickets are sold that is near to 615.

So, first usher guess was better.

11. **(C)**

Number of pieces of plywood $= \dfrac{1.89\,\text{m}}{0.35\,\text{cm}}$

$= \dfrac{1.89 \times 100\,\text{cm}}{0.35\,\text{cm}}$

$= \dfrac{\frac{189}{100}}{\frac{35}{100}} = \dfrac{189 \times 100}{35}$

$= \dfrac{189 \times 20}{7}$

$= 27 \times 20 = 540$

12. **(B)**

Distance covered in 5 litres of petrol

$$= \frac{31.8}{2.4} \times 5 = \frac{318}{24} \times 5$$

$$= 66.25 \text{ km}$$

13. **(C)**

Let the polygon has n sides.

$3.9 \times n = 31.2$

$$\Rightarrow n = \frac{31.2}{3.9} = \frac{312}{39} = 8$$

14. **(C)**

$0.4 \div 0.4 \div 0.4$

$$\frac{4}{10} \div \frac{4}{10} \div \frac{4}{10} = \frac{4}{10} \times \frac{10}{4} \times \frac{10}{4}$$

$$= \frac{10}{4} = 2.5$$

15. **(C)**

Cost per litre $= \dfrac{1550.50}{17.5} = ₹88.6$

16. **(D)**

Distance = Speed × Time

$$\text{Speed} = \frac{\text{Distance}}{\text{Time}} = \frac{31.25}{\frac{1}{2}} = 31.25 \times 2$$

$$= 62.5 \text{ km}$$

Distance $= 62.5 \times 16 = 1000$ km

17. **(A)**

$(0.25)2 - (0.19)2$

$$= 0.0625 - 0.0361$$

$$= 0.0264$$

18. **(D)**

$11.1 \times 1.1 \times 0.11 = 1.3431$

19. **(A)**

$100 - (27.75 + 4.25 + 26.45)$

$$= 100 - 58.45 = 41.55$$

20. **(A)**

$(79.1 + 18.07) - (27.73 + 46.37)$

$$= 97.17 - 74.1 = 23.07$$

HOTS (ACHIEVERS SECTION)

21. (A)	22. (B)	23. (D)	24. (B)	25. (D)

3. DATA HANDLING

Answer Key

1. (B)	2. (A)	3. (B)	4. (B)	5. (C)	6. (B)	7. (C)	8. (C)	9. (C)	10. (C)
11. (B)	12. (C)	13. (B)	14. (C)	15. (D)	16. (A)	17. (D)	18. (B)	19. (B)	20. (C)

1. **(B)**

First 15 odd numbers are 3, 5, 7, 9, 11, 13, 15, 17, 19, 21, 23, 25, 27, 29, 31.

n = 15, which is odd.

$$\text{Median} = \left(\frac{15+1}{2}\right)th \text{ term} = 8\text{th term} = 17$$

2. **(A)**

$n = 50$, which is even.

$$\text{Median} = \left[\frac{50}{2}th \text{ term} + \left(\frac{50}{2}+1\right)th \text{ term}\right]$$

$$= \frac{1}{2}\left[25th \text{ term} + 26th \text{ term}\right]$$

$$= \frac{1}{2}[25 + 26] = \frac{51}{2} = 25.5$$

3. (B)
The numbers in the ascending order are 7, 8, 9, 15, 16, 19, 21, 22, 23, 28, 40
$n = 11$, which is odd.

$$\text{Median} = \left(\frac{11+1}{2}\right)\text{th term} = \text{6th term} = 19.$$

4. (B)
As 28 appears two times, but other numbers appear only once.

5. (C)
Mode $= 3$ Median $- 2$ Mean
$$= 3\,(51) - 2\,(50)$$
$$= 153 - 100$$
$$= 53 \text{ kg}$$

6. (B)
Mode $= 22.16$
Median $= 22$
Mode $= 3$ Median $- 2$ Mean
$22.16 = 3 \times 22 - 2$ Mean
2 Mean $= 66 - 22.16 = 43.84$

$$\text{Mean} = \frac{43.84}{2} = 21.92$$

7. (C)
Mean $=$
$$\frac{7+14+21+28+35+42+49+56+63+70+77+84}{12}$$

$$= \frac{546}{12} = 45.5$$

8. (C)

Marks	No. of students	Cumulative frequency
15	3	3
17	5	8
20	9	17
22	4	21
25	6	27
30	10	37

$N = 37$
$N = 37$, which is odd.

$$\text{Median} = \left(\frac{37+1}{2}\right)\text{th} = \text{19th term} = 22$$

9. (C)

Wt. in kg (x_i)	No. of labours (f_i)	$x_i f_i$
60	4	240
63	5	315
65	4	260
72	2	144
75	6	450
77	3	231

$\Sigma f_i = 24 \qquad \Sigma x_i f_i = 1640$

$$\text{Mean} = \frac{\Sigma x_i f_i}{\Sigma f_i} = \frac{1640}{24} = 68.33$$

10. (C)
First 9 multiples of 12 are 12, 24, 36, 48, 60, 72, 84, 96, 108
$n = 9$
$$\text{Median} = \left(\frac{9+1}{2}\right)\text{th} = \text{5th term} = 60$$

11. (B)
Mode $= 27$, as it occurs 3 times.

12. (C)
$$\frac{16+24+x+34+35+25+37+42+47}{9}$$
$$= 32$$
$$\Rightarrow 260 + x = 288 \qquad \Rightarrow x = 288 - 260 = 28$$

13. (B)
The height in ascending order are 160, 164, 165, 168, 170, 171, 173, 174, 182.
$n = 9$, which is odd.
$$\text{Median} = \left(\frac{9+1}{2}\right)\text{th} = \text{5th term} = 170 \text{ cm.}$$

14. (C)
Mean $=$
$$\frac{45\times5+27\times3+20\times8+56\times7+82\times2+75\times4+17\times12}{5+3+8+7+2+4+12}$$

$$= \frac{225+81+160+392+164+300+204}{41}$$

$$= \frac{1526}{41} = 37.219 \approx 37.22$$

15. (D)

Marks obtained	No. of students	Cumulative frequency
42	3	3
47	8	11
52	6	17
57	8	25
62	11	36
67	5	41
72	9	50

$N = 50$

$N = 50$, which is even.

$$\text{Median} = \frac{\left(\frac{50}{2}\right)th \ \text{term} + \left(\frac{50}{2}+1\right)th \ \text{term}}{2}$$

$$\text{Median} = \frac{25th \ \text{term} + 26th \ \text{term}}{2}$$

$$= \frac{57+62}{2} = \frac{119}{2} = 59.5$$

16. (A)

The ages in the ascending order are 24, 28, 32, 37, 38, 41, 42, 43, 45, 47, 48, 49, 50, 51, 56,

Range $= 56 - 24 = 32$

17. (D)

Arithmetic Mean

$$= \frac{59+36+57+35+60+55+46+50}{8}$$

$$= \frac{398}{8} = 49.75$$

18. (B)

The frequency of 2 is highest.

So, mode $= 2$

19. (B)

The marks in ascending order are 12, 17, 19, 27, 36, 38, 39, 42, 47, 48, 61, 65, 68, 78, 84.

$n = 15$, which is odd.

$$\text{Median} = \left(\frac{15+1}{2}\right)th = 8\text{th term} = 42$$

20. (C)

Mode $= 15$

HOTS (ACHIEVERS SECTION)

21. (A)	22. (C)	23. (A)	24. (A)	25. (C)

4. SIMPLE EQUATIONS

Answer Key

1. (C)	2. (B)	3. (B)	4. (A)	5. (B)	6. (D)	7. (C)	8. (C)	9. (A)	10. (B)
11. (C)	12. (D)	13. (D)	14. (A)	15. (A)	16. (D)	17. (B)	18. (A)	19. (B)	20. (B)

1. (C)

Let the total property be ` x.

$$x - \left(\frac{x}{3}+\frac{x}{4}\right) = 18000$$

$$\Rightarrow \quad x - \frac{x}{3} - \frac{x}{4} = 18000$$

$$\Rightarrow \quad 5x = 12 \times 18000$$

$$\Rightarrow \quad x = \frac{12 \times 18000}{5} = ₹43200$$

2. (B)

Let total marks be x.

Pass marks $= 40\%$ of $x = \dfrac{40x}{100}$

$$\therefore \quad \frac{40x}{100} = 185 + 15$$

$$\Rightarrow \quad x = \frac{200 \times 100}{40} = 500$$

3. (B)

Quantity of nickel in 50 kg of alloy

$$= 60\% \text{ of } 50 \text{ kg} = 30 \text{ kg}$$

Let the required quantity of lead = x kg

Weight of new alloy = $(30 + x)$ kg

$$\therefore \quad \frac{30 + x}{50 + x} \times 100 = 75 \quad \Rightarrow \quad \frac{30 + x}{50 + x} = \frac{3}{4}$$

$$\Rightarrow 120 + 4x = 150 + 3x$$

$$\Rightarrow \quad 4x - 3x = 150 - 120 \Rightarrow x = 30$$

4. (A)

Let unit's digit be x.

Ten's digit = $(9 - x)$

Number = $10(9 - x) + 1 \times x = 90 - 10x + x$

$$\therefore \quad 90 - 9x + 27 = x \times 10 + (9 - x)1.$$

$$\Rightarrow \quad 117 - 9x = 10x + 9 - x$$

$$\Rightarrow \quad 117 - 9x = 9x + 9$$

$$\Rightarrow 18x = 108 \Rightarrow x = \frac{108}{18} = 6$$

$$\therefore \quad \text{Number} = 90 - 9 \times 6 = 90 - 54 = 36$$

5. (B)

Given $x - \left(2x - \dfrac{3x - 4}{7}\right) = \dfrac{4x - 27}{3} - 3$

$$\Rightarrow x - 2x + \frac{3x - 4}{7} = \frac{4x - 27}{3} - 3$$

$$\Rightarrow \frac{7x - 2x + 3x - 4}{7} = \frac{4x - 27 - 9}{3}$$

$$\Rightarrow \quad 24x - 12 = 28x - 252$$

$$\Rightarrow \quad 4x = -12 + 252$$

$$\Rightarrow \quad 4x = 240 \Rightarrow x = \frac{240}{4} = 60$$

6. (D)

Let the cost price be ₹x.

$$\therefore \quad x + 5\% \text{ of } x = 714$$

$$\Rightarrow \quad x + \frac{5x}{100} = 174$$

$$\Rightarrow \quad 105x = 714 \times 100$$

$$\Rightarrow \quad x = \frac{714 \times 100}{105} = 34 \times 20 = ₹680$$

7. (C)

Let the breadth of rectangle = x

Length = $3x$

Perimeter of rectangle = 128

$$\therefore \quad 2(x + 3x) = 128$$

$$\Rightarrow \quad 4x = \frac{128}{2}$$

$$\Rightarrow \quad 4x = 64$$

$$\Rightarrow \quad x = \frac{64}{4} = 16$$

$$\therefore \quad \text{Length} = 3 \times 16 = 48m$$

8. (C)

Let the total journey be x km.

$$\therefore \quad \frac{3x}{5} + \frac{x}{4} + \frac{x}{8} + 4 = x$$

$$\Rightarrow \quad \frac{24x + 10x + 5x + 160}{40} = x$$

$$\Rightarrow \quad 39x + 160 = 40x$$

$$\Rightarrow \quad x = 160$$

9. (A)

Let the unit's digit be x.

10's digit = $8 - x$.

Number = $10(8 - x) + 1 \times x = 80 - 10x + x$

$$= 80 - 9x$$

and $80 - 9x + 18 = 10 \times x + (8 - x) 1$

$$\Rightarrow 98 - 9x = 10x + 8 - x$$

$$\Rightarrow 98 - 9x = 9x + 8$$

$$\Rightarrow 18x = 90 \qquad \Rightarrow x = \frac{90}{18} = 5$$

Number = $80 - 9 \times 5 = 80 - 45 = 35$

10. (B)

Let the number be x

$$\therefore \quad x - 21 = 71 - x$$

$$\Rightarrow x + x = 71 + 21$$

$$\Rightarrow 2x = 92$$

$$\Rightarrow x = \frac{92}{2} = 46$$

11. (C)

Let the smaller angle be x.

$\therefore$ Other angle $= x + 20°$

Now $x + x + 20° = 180°$

$\Rightarrow \quad 2x = 160°$

$\Rightarrow \quad x = 80°$

12. (D)

Let the number be x.

$\therefore \quad 5x = x + 80$

$\Rightarrow 5x - x = 80$

$\Rightarrow \quad 4x = 80$

$\Rightarrow \quad x = \dfrac{80}{4} = 20$

13. (D)

Let the three consecutive odd numbers be x, $x + 2$, $x + 4$.

$\therefore \quad x + x + 2 + x + 4 = 99$

$\Rightarrow \quad 3x + 6 = 99$

$\Rightarrow \quad 3x = 93$

$\Rightarrow \quad x = 31$

$\therefore$ The numbers are 31, 33, 35

Hence, difference $= 35 - 31 = 4$

14. (A)

Let Simran's age $= 5x$

Ranjana's age $= 3x$

After 6 years, Simran's age $= 5x + 6$

Ranjana's age $= 3x + 6$

$\therefore \quad \dfrac{5x + 6}{3x + 6} = \dfrac{7}{5}$

$\Rightarrow 25x + 30 = 21x + 42$

$\Rightarrow 25x - 21x = 42 - 30$

$\Rightarrow 4x = 12$

$\Rightarrow x = \dfrac{12}{4} = 3$

$\therefore$ Present age of Ranjana $= 3x$

$= 3 \times 3 = 9$ years

15. (A)

Let the number be x.

$\therefore \quad 3x + 6 = 84$

$\Rightarrow \quad 3x = 84 - 6$

$\Rightarrow \quad 3x = 78$

$\Rightarrow \quad x = \dfrac{78}{3} = 26$

16. (D)

Let the two consecutive even number be x and $x + 2$.

$\therefore \quad x + x + 2 = 98$

$\Rightarrow \quad 2x + 2 = 98$

$\Rightarrow \quad 2x = 98 - 2$

$\Rightarrow \quad 2x = 96$

$\Rightarrow \quad x = \dfrac{96}{2} = 48$

17. (B)

Let the whole number be x.

$\therefore \quad 2x + 9 = 61$

$\Rightarrow \quad 2x = 61 - 9$

$\Rightarrow \quad 2x = 52$

$\Rightarrow \quad x = \dfrac{52}{2} = 26$

Hence, $\dfrac{5}{13}$ of $26 = 10$

18. (A)

Let the present age be x years.

$\therefore$ 4 years ago, his age $= (x - 4)$ years.

After 12 years, his age $= (x + 12)$ years.

Hence, $x + 12 = 3(x - 4)$

$\Rightarrow x + 12 = 3x - 12$

$\Rightarrow 2x = 24 \Rightarrow x = \dfrac{24}{2} = 12$ years.

19. (B)

Let the present age of Niraj be x years.

His cousin's age $= x + 19$

After 5 years,

$\dfrac{x + 5}{x + 19 + 5} = \dfrac{2}{3} \Rightarrow 3x + 15 = 2x + 48$

$\Rightarrow 3x - 2x = 48 - 15$

$\Rightarrow \quad x = 33$

20. (B)

Given $8(2p - 5) - 6(3p - 7) = 1$

$\Rightarrow 16p - 40 - 18p + 42 = 1$

$\Rightarrow \quad -2p + 2 = 1$

$\Rightarrow \quad -2p = 1 - 2$

$\Rightarrow \quad -2p = -1$

$\Rightarrow \quad p = \dfrac{1}{2}$

21. (A)	22. (A)	23. (A)	24. (C)	25. (D)

5. LINES AND ANGLES

Answer Key

1. (C)	2. (B)	3. (A)	4. (B)	5. (C)	6. (C)	7. (B)	8. (B)	9. (B)	10. (B)
11. (A)	12. (C)	13. (B)	14. (C)	15. (B)	16. (C)	17. (B)	18. (A)	19. (A)	20. (C)

1. (C)
$180° - 64° = 116°$

2. (A)
$64 + x + 93 = 180$
$\Rightarrow \quad 157 + x = 180°$
$\Rightarrow \quad x = 180° - 157° = 23°$

3. (A)

4. (B)

5. (C)

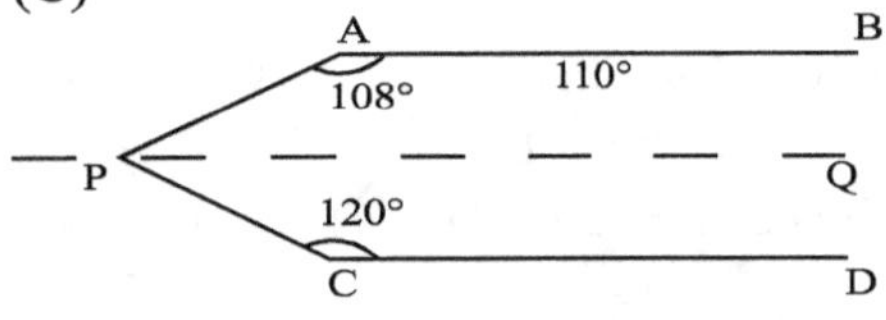

$AB \parallel PQ$
$\therefore \ \angle APQ = 180° - 108° = 72°$
$PQ \parallel CD$
$\angle CPQ = 180° - 120° = 60°$
$\angle APC = \angle APQ + \angle CPQ = 72° + 60°$
$\qquad\qquad\quad = 132°$

6. (C)

Given, $MN \parallel PQ$
$\angle PON = 100°$
$\therefore \ \angle NOE = 180° - 100 = 80°$
$\angle ENO = 180° - 120° = 60°$
$\qquad x = 180° - (80° + 60°)$
$\quad = 180° - 140° = 40°$

7. (B)
$5x + 7x = 180°$
$\Rightarrow 12x = 180° \Rightarrow x = \dfrac{180°}{12} = 15°$

$\angle 1 = 5x = 5 \times 15 = 75°$
$\angle 2 = 7x = 7 \times 15 = 105°$
$\angle 1 = \angle 5 = 75°$
$\angle 8 = 180° - 75° = 105°$

8. (B) Here, $2x - 10° + 3x + 20° = 180°$
$\Rightarrow 5x + 10° = 180°$
$\Rightarrow 5x = 170°$
$\Rightarrow x = \dfrac{170°}{5} = 34°$

9. (B)
$x + x = 90° \Rightarrow 2x = 90° \Rightarrow x = \dfrac{90°}{2} = 45°$

10. (B)

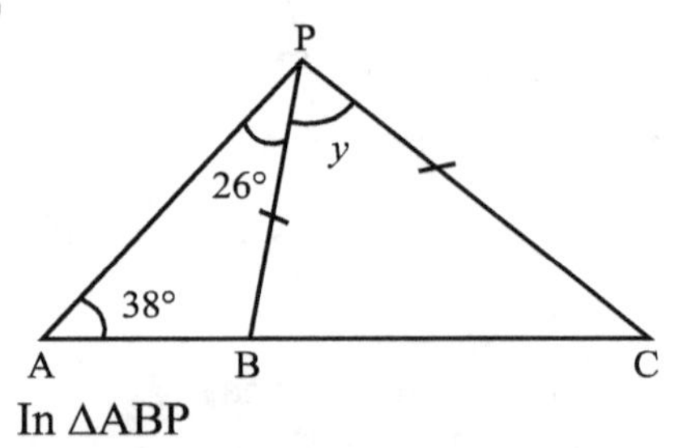

In $\triangle ABP$
$\angle ABP = 180° - (26° + 38°)$
$\qquad\qquad = 180° - 64 = 116°$
$\angle PBC = 180° - 116° = 64°$
$PB = PC$
$\angle PBC = 64°$
$y = 180° - (64° + 64°)$
$\quad = 180° - 128°$
$\quad = 52°$

11. **(A)**

$x + 45° = 84°$

$x = 84° - 45° = 39°$

12. **(C)**

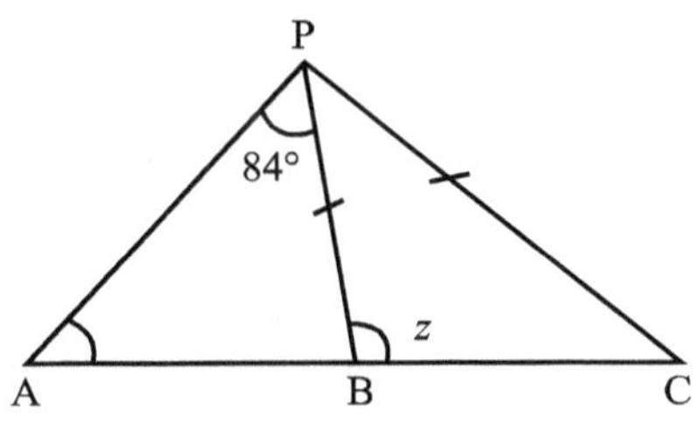

In $\triangle$ PAB,

$\angle PAB + \angle PBP + 84° = 180°$

$\angle PBA + \angle PBA = 180° - 84°$

$2 \angle PBA = 96°$

$\angle PBA = \dfrac{96°}{2} = 48°$

$z + 48° = 180° \Rightarrow z = 180° - 48 = 132°$

13. **(B)**

$AB = AC$

$\Rightarrow 5x + 1 = 2x + 13$

$\Rightarrow 5x - 2x = 13 - 1$

$\Rightarrow 3x = 12 \Rightarrow x = \dfrac{12}{3} = 4$

and $BC = 2x - 3 = 2 \times 4 - 3 = 5$

14. **(C)**

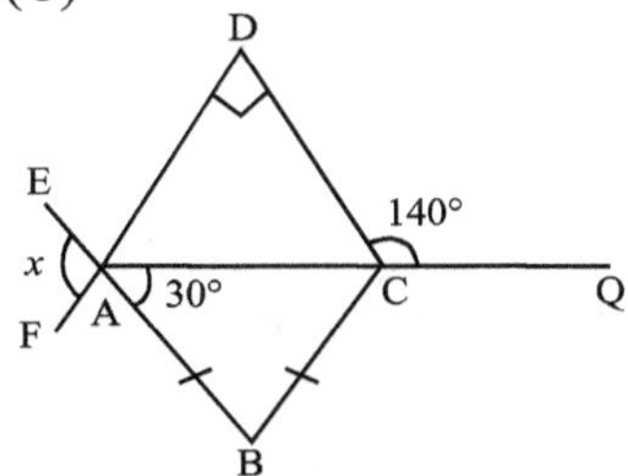

In $\triangle ACD$

$\angle DAC = 180° - 140°$

$\qquad = 40°$

$\angle DAC = 180° - (90° + 40°)$

$\qquad = 50°$

$\angle DAB = 50° + 30°$

$\qquad = 80°$

$x = \angle DAB = 80°$

15. **(B)**

Perimeter of triangle ABC = 78

$\therefore 2x - 3 + 7x - 5 + 5x + 2 = 78$

$\Rightarrow 14x - 6 = 78$

$\Rightarrow 14x = 78 + 6$

$\Rightarrow 14x = 84 \Rightarrow x = \dfrac{84}{14} = 6$

Sides are $5x + 2 = 5 \times 6 + 2 = 32$

$7x - 5 = 7 \times 6 - 5 = 37$

$2x - 3 = 2 \times 6 - 3 = 9$

16. **(C)**

$\angle ABC = \angle ACB = 60°$

At point C,

$x + 60° = 180°$

$\Rightarrow x = 180° - 60° \Rightarrow \qquad x = 120°$

17. **(B)**

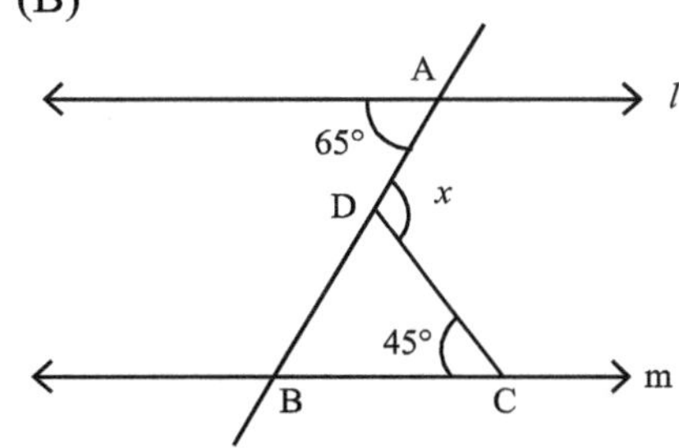

$\angle DBC = 65°$ as $l \parallel m$.

$\angle BDC = 180° - (65° + 45°)$

$\angle BDC = 180° - 110° = 70°$

$x = 180° - 70° = 110°$

18. **(A)**

$\dfrac{y}{x} = 5 \Rightarrow y = 5x, \quad \dfrac{z}{x} = 4 \Rightarrow z = 4x$

Now $x + y + z = 180°$

$\Rightarrow x + 5x + 4x = 180° \Rightarrow 10x = 180°$

$\Rightarrow x = \dfrac{180}{10} = 18°$

19. **(A)**

At point O,

$78° + 50° + 90° + 40° + 30° + x = 360°$

$\Rightarrow 288° + x = 360°$

$x = 360° - 288° = 72°$

20. **(C)**

BA ∥ CE

    $\angle BAC = \angle ACE = 56°$

    At point C,

$\Rightarrow \angle ACB + \angle ACE + \angle ECD = 180°$

$\Rightarrow \angle ACB + 56° + 73° = 180°$

$\Rightarrow \angle ACB = 180° - (56° + 73°)$

$\Rightarrow \angle ACB \qquad = 180° - 129° = 51°$

<table>
<tr><td colspan="5">HOTS (ACHIEVERS SECTION)</td></tr>
<tr><td>21. (A)</td><td>22. (C)</td><td>23. (A)</td><td>24. (B)</td><td>25. (C)</td></tr>
</table>

6. THE TRIANGLES & PROPERTIES

Answer Key

1. (B)	2. (A)	3. (D)	4. (A)	5. (C)	6. (D)	7. (B)	8. (C)	9. (D)	10. (B)
11. (B)	12. (C)	13. (A)	14. (B)	15. (C)	16. (B)	17. (D)	18. (B)	19. (D)	20. (B)

1. (B)

Let the measure of each unknown angle be $x°$. We know that the sum of the angles of a triangle is 180°.

$\therefore x + x + 70 = 180°$

$\Rightarrow 2x = (180° - 70°)$

$\Rightarrow 2x = 110°$

$\Rightarrow x = 55°$

Hence each unknown angle is 55°.

2. (A)

We know that the sum of the angles of a triangle is 180°.

$\therefore \angle X + \angle Y + \angle Z = 180°$

$\Rightarrow 90° + \angle Y + 48° = 180°$

$\Rightarrow \angle Y = 180° - 138°$

$\Rightarrow \angle Y = 42°$

3. (D)

Let the third angle be $x°$.

We know that the sum of the angles of a triangle is 180°.

$\therefore 2x + 2x + x = 180°$

$\Rightarrow 5x = 180°$

$\Rightarrow x = 36°$

So, the angles are $(2 × 36)°$, $(2 × 36)°$ and $(x)°$

Hence, the angles of the triangles are 72°, 72°, 36°.

4. (A)

All the angles of equilateral triangle are equal.

5. (C)

Let the measure of the given angles of the triangle be $(4x)°$, $(3x)°$ and $(2x)°$ respectively.

$4x + 3x + 2x = 180°$

$\Rightarrow 9x = 180°$

$\Rightarrow x = \dfrac{180°}{9} = 20°$

So, the angles measure $(4×20)°$, $(3 × 20)°$ and $(2 × 20)°$

Hence, the angles of the triangle are 80°, 60°, 40°.

6. (D)

We know that an exterior angle of a triangle is equal to the sum of its interior opposite angles.

$\therefore \angle ABC + \angle BAC = \angle ACD$

$\Rightarrow 55° + x = 125°$

$\Rightarrow x = (125 - 55) = 70°$

Also, we know that the sum of all the angles of a triangle is 180°.

$\therefore x + y + 55 = 180° \Rightarrow 70 + y + 55 - 180$

$\Rightarrow 125 + y = 180$

$\Rightarrow y = 180 - 125 = 55$

Hence, $x = 70$ and $y = 55$

7. **(B)**

We know that an exterior angle of a triangle is equal to the sum of its interior opposite angles.

$$\therefore \angle ABC + \angle BAC = \angle ACD$$
$$\Rightarrow \qquad 68° + x = 130°$$
$$\Rightarrow \qquad x = (130° - 68°) = 62°$$

The sum of all the angles of a triangle is 180°.
$$x + y + 68 = 180° \Rightarrow 62° + y + 68° = 180°$$
$$\Rightarrow 130° + y = 180°$$
$$y = 180° - 130°$$
$$= 50°$$

8. **(C)**

Let $x = 2t$, $y = 3t$, then $2t + 3t = 130° \Rightarrow t = 26°$
$$\Rightarrow \quad x = 2 \times 26 = 52°$$
and $y = 3 \times 26 = 78°$
$$z = 50°$$
$\therefore$ Sum of all angles of a triangle is 180°.

9. **(D)**

Let O be the initial position of the man. Let he cover OA = 24m due east and then AB = 10m due north.

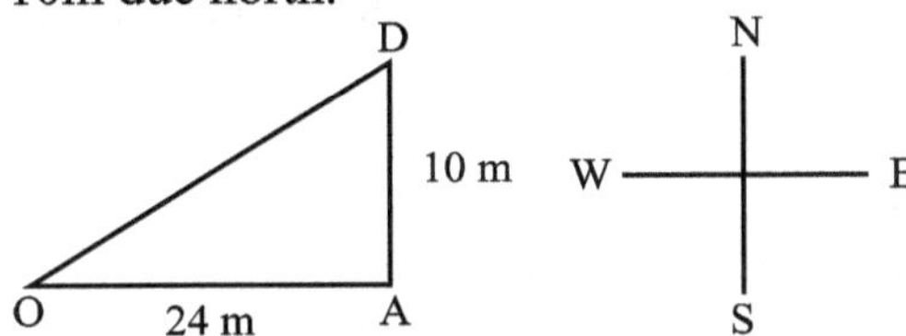

Finally, he reaches the point B. Join OB.
$$OB^2 = (OA^2 + OB^2) = \{(24)^2 + (10)^2\}\ m^2$$
$$= (576 + 100)\ m^2 = 676\ m^2$$
$$\Rightarrow \quad OB = \sqrt{676}\ m = 26\ m$$

Hence, the man is at a distance at 26m from his initial position.

10. **(B)**

(i) Here $a = 8$ cm, $b = 5$cm and $c = 10c$,
The largest side is $c = 10$cm.
$$a^2 + b^2 = \{(8)^2 + (5)^2\}\ cm^2$$
$$= m\ (64 + 25)\ cm^2 = 89\ cm^2 \neq (10)^2\ cm^2$$
$$a^2 + b^2 \neq c^2$$
$\therefore$ Given triangle is not right angled.

(ii) Here $a = 7$ cm, $b = 24$ cm and $c = 25$ cm
The largest side is $c = 25$ cm
$$a^2 + b^2 = \{(7)^2 + (24)^2\}\ cm^2 = (49 + 576)\ cm^2$$
$$= 625\ cm^2 = (25\ cm)^2 = c^2$$
$$\Rightarrow a^2 + b^2 = c^2$$
Given triangle is right angled.

11. **(B)**

Let AB and CD be the given poles such that AB = 9 m, CD = 14 m and AC = 12 m. Join BD.

From B, draw BL $\perp$ CD.
$$DL = (CD - CL) = (CD - AB)$$
$$= (14 - 9)\ m = 5\ m$$

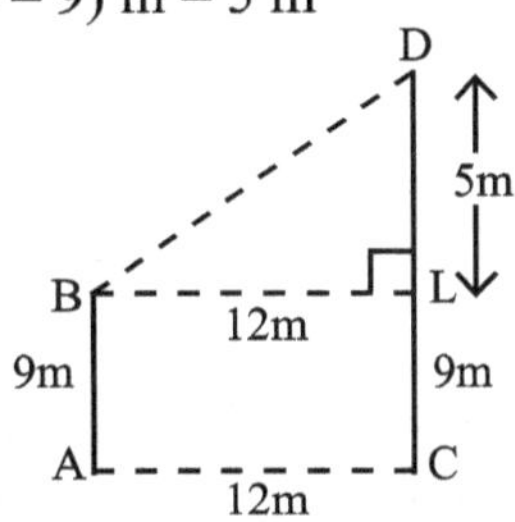

BL = AC = 12 m
Now, in right ΔBLD, by Pythagoras theorem. We have
$$BD^2 = BL^2 + DL^2 = \{(12)^2 + (5)^2\}m^2$$
$$= (144 + 25)\ m^2 = 169\ m^2$$
$$\Rightarrow \quad BD = \sqrt{169}\ m = \sqrt{13 \times 13}\ m = 13\ m$$

14. **(B)**

We know that the sum of the angles of a triangle is 180°.
$$\therefore\ \angle A + \angle B + \angle C = 180°$$
$$\Rightarrow \quad \angle A = 180° - 66° \qquad \Rightarrow \angle A = 114°$$

16. **(B)**

$\angle A = 33° + \angle B$ and $\angle C = \angle B - 18°$
$$\therefore\ (33° + \angle B) + \angle B + (\angle B - 18°) = 180°$$
$$\Rightarrow\ 3\angle B = 165° \Rightarrow \qquad \angle B = 55°$$

17. **(D)**

The sum of all the angles of a triangle is 180°.

19. **(D)**

Here, $(3x - 8)° + 50° + (x + 10)° = 180°$
$$\Rightarrow 4x + 52 = 180°$$

$\Rightarrow 4x = 180 - 52$

$\Rightarrow x = \dfrac{128}{4}$

$\Rightarrow x = 32$

20. (B)

By Pythagoras theorem,

$AB^2 + BC^2 = AC^2 \Rightarrow 5^2 + BC^2 = 132$

$\Rightarrow BC^2 = \sqrt{13^2 - 5^2} = \sqrt{169 - 25} = \sqrt{144}$

$= 12$ cm

<table>
<tr><td colspan="5" align="center">HOTS (ACHIEVERS SECTION)</td></tr>
<tr><td>21. (C)</td><td>22. (B)</td><td>23. (A)</td><td>24. (A)</td><td>25. (C)</td></tr>
</table>

7. CONGRUENCE OF TRIANGLES

Answer Key

1. (D)	2. (B)	3. (D)	4. (D)	5. (A)	6. (C)	7. (C)	8. (D)	9. (C)	10. (A)
11. (B)	12. (A)	13. (C)	14. (C)	15. (B)	16. (A)	17. (C)	18. (A)	19. (A)	20. (D)

1. **(D)**

   The vertex of the angle is the point where the two sides of the angle meet. These would be the sides that include the angle. So when the vertex A and vertex B meets the side AB is formed it means there is side AB between the angle A and angle B.

2. **(B)**

   As per the congruency of triangles: BAC $\leftrightarrow$ RPQ, then PR = AB QR = CB QP = CA

3. **(D)**

   Under the correspondence: ABC $\leftrightarrow$ RQP then $\angle B = \angle Q$ $\angle A = \angle R$ $\angle C = \angle P$

4. **(D)**

   Under the correspondence: ABC $\leftrightarrow$ RQP then, then, $\angle A = \angle R$ $\angle B = \angle Q$ $\angle C = \angle P$

5. **(A)**

   If $\triangle DEF \cong \triangle ACB$ then, $\angle D = \angle A$ $\angle E = \angle C$ $\angle F = \angle B$

6. **(C)**

   As per the congruency of triangles: BCA $\leftrightarrow$ RPQ, then RP = BC PQ = CA RQ = BA

7. **(C)**

   As per the congruency of triangles: ABC $\leftrightarrow$ RPQ, then AB=RP BC = PQ AC=RQ

8. **(D)**

   Let the angles of the triangle be a, b and c. According to question, $a = b + c$ Now, sum of angles of a triangle $= 180°$ $a + b + c = 180°$ $a + a = 180°$ $a = 90°$ Therefore, one angle of the triangle will be right angle. Hence, D is the correct answer.

9. **(C)**

   Let the third side be c. We know that the sum of two sides of a triangle is always greater than the third side, Therefore, $4 + c > 8$ $c > 4$ Also, $4 + 8 > c$ $c < 12$ Therefore, $4 <$ Third side < 12 Hence, C is the correct answer.

10. **(A)**

    Let the equal sides be x. Now, we know according to the Pythagoras theorem, the sum of the square of sides equal to the square of largest side. Therefore, $x^2 + x^2 = (4)^2$ $2 \times 2 = 16$ $x^2 = 8$ $x = 2\sqrt{2}$ cm Hence, A is the correct answer.

11. **(B)**

    In a right-angled triangle, the sum of the square of two sides of a right-angled triangle equals the square of the largest side. Therefore, $x^2 + y^2 = z^2$ $x^2 + y^2 - z^2 = 0$ Hence, B is the correct answer.

12. **(A)**

OLYMPIAD WORKBOOK (IMO) CLASS – 7

In a triangle, the sum of two sides is always greater than the third side. Therefore, $a + b > c$ $a + c > b$ $b + c > a$ Hence, A is the correct answer.

13. **(C)**

In a triangle, the sum of two sides is always greater than the third side. Therefore, $x + 6 > 8$ $x > 2$ Also, $8 + 6 > x$ $x < 14$ So, $2 < x < 14$ Hence, C is the correct answer.

15. **(B)**

We can conclude CA = ED, AB = DF, CB = EF, $\angle$CAB = $\angle$EDF, $\angle$ACB = $\angle$DEF, $\angle$ABC = $\angle$DFE

16. **(A)**

The sides corresponding to AC and DE respectively are DF and AB.

$\therefore$ AC = 10 cm, and DE = 3 cm.

17. **(C)**

Two equilateral triangles of the same length of their sides are congruent

18. **(A)**

If the three angles of a triangle are congruent to corresponding angles of the other, it is an enlarged copy of the triangle.

19. **(A)**

Since, AB = AC $\Rightarrow$ 1/2AB = 1/2AC

$\Rightarrow$ BF = EC

Also, AB = AC $\Rightarrow$ $\angle$B

= $\angle$C [Angles opposite to equal sides are equal]

In $\triangle$ BEC and $\triangle$ CFB EC = FB

$\angle$B = $\angle$C

BC = BC

$\therefore \triangle$BEC $\cong \triangle$CFB

$\Rightarrow$ BE = CF

<table><tr><td colspan="5" align="center">HOTS (ACHIEVERS SECTION)</td></tr><tr><td>21. (D)</td><td>22. (C)</td><td>23. (D)</td><td>24. (D)</td><td>25. (D)</td></tr></table>

21. **(D)**

In $\triangle$ ABD and $\triangle$ CDB

AD = BC

$\angle$BDA = $\angle$DBC (Alternate angles)

BD = BD

Therefore $\triangle$ ABD $\cong \triangle$ CDB (By SAS postulate)

22. **(C)**

In $\triangle$ABC and $\triangle$DBC,

$\angle$ABC = $\angle$BCD

AC = BD (Given)

BC = BC (Common Side)

$\triangle$ABC $\cong \triangle$DCB WCB (By RHS postulate)

23. **(D)**

In $\triangle$ADB and $\triangle$ACB

AD = BC   (Given)

AC = BD

AB = BA   (Common)

therefore $\triangle$ADB $\cong \triangle$ACB

$\angle$ABD = $\angle$CAB

$\angle$ABP = $\angle$PAB

PA = PB (Sides opp. equal angles are qual)

$\triangle$PAB is isosceles.

24. **(D)**

In PQR and PSR

PS = QR, PQ = SR, PR = PR

RQP $\cong$ RSP (By SSS postulate)

25. **(D)**

Clearly, $\angle$WXY corresponds to $\angle$BCD because BC faces the angles marked with one arc and three arc and XY also faces the angles marked with one arc and three arcs.

So, D is the correct option.

8. COMPARING QUANTITIES

1. (A)	2. (D)	3. (D)	4. (D)	5. (A)	6. (A)	7. (B)	8. (C)	9. (A)	10. (B)
11. (B)	12. (B)	13. (B)	14. (B)	15. (C)	16. (A)	17. (C)	18. (C)	19. (C)	20. (D)
21. (A)	22. (A)	23. (A)	24. (C)	25. (B)	26. (D)	27. (B)	28. (C)	29. (B)	30. (D)

1. (A)
20% of $a = b$
$\Rightarrow (20/100)a = b$
$\therefore b\%$ of $20 = (b/100) \times 20$
$\quad = [(20/100)a \times (1/100) \times 20]$
$\quad = (4/100)a = 4\%$ of a

2. (D)
Let the number of students be x. Then,
Number of students who are 8 years and above
$= (100 - 20)\%$ of $x = 80\%$ of x.
$\therefore \qquad 80\%$ of $x = 48 + 2/3$ of 48
$\Rightarrow \qquad (80/100)\, x = 80$
$\Rightarrow \qquad x = 100$

3. (D)
5% of A + 4% of B
$= 2/3$ (6% of A + 8% of B)
$\Rightarrow (5/100)A + (4/100)B$
$= 2/3[(6/100)A + (8/100)B]$
$\Rightarrow (1/20)A + (1/25)B = (1/25)A + (4/75)B$
$\Rightarrow (1/20 - 1/25)A = (4/75 - 1/25)B$
$\Rightarrow (1/100)A = (1/75)$ B
$A/B = 100/75 = 4/3$
$\therefore$ Required ratio $= 4 : 3$

4. (D)
Let the number be x.
Then, error $= (5/3)\, x - (3/5)\, x = (16/15)\, x$.
Error% $= [(16x/15) \times (3/5x) \times 100]\%$
$\quad = 64\%$

5. (A)
Number of valid votes $= 80\%$ of 7500
$\qquad\qquad = 6000$
$\therefore$ Valid votes polled by other candidates
$= 45\%$ of $6000 = (45/100 \times 6000) = 2700$

6. (A)
Total number of votes polled
$= (1136 + 7636 + 11628) = 20400$
$\therefore$ Required percentage
$= [(11628/20400) \times 100]\% = 57\%$

7. (B)
Let the sum paid to Y per week be ₹z.
Then, $z + 120\%$ of $z = 550$.
$\Rightarrow z + (120/100)\, z = 550$
$\Rightarrow (11/5)\, z = 550$
$\Rightarrow z = (550 \times 5)/11 = 250$

8. (C)
Let the amount on taxable purchases be ₹x.
Then, 6% of $x = 30/100$
$\Rightarrow x = [(30/100) \times (100/6)] = 5$
$\therefore$ Cost of tax free items
$= ₹[25 - (5 + 0.30)] = ₹19.70$

9. (A)
Rebate $= 6\%$ of ₹$6650 = ₹399$.
Sales tax $= 10\%$ of ₹$(6650 - 399)$
$\qquad\qquad = ₹625.10$
$\therefore$ Final amount $= ₹(6251 + 625.10)$
$\qquad\qquad = ₹6876.10$

10. (B)
Increase in 10 years $= (262500 - 175000)$
$\qquad\qquad = 87500$
Increase% $= [(87500/175000) \times 100]\%$
$\quad = 50\%$
$\therefore$ Required average $= (50/10)\% = 5\%$

11. (B)
Cost Price (C.P.) $= ₹(4700 + 800)$
$\qquad\qquad = ₹5500$
Selling Price (S.P.) $= ₹5800$
Gain $= $ (S.P.) $-$ (C.P.) $= ₹(5800 - 5500)$
$\qquad\qquad = ₹300$

Gain % = (300/5500) × 100% = $5\frac{5}{11}$%

12. (B)

Let C.P. of each article be ₹1, C.P. of x articles = ₹x

S.P. of x articles = ₹20

Profit = ₹$(20 - x)$

Therefore, $(20 - x)/x × 100 = 25$

$\Rightarrow 2000 - 100x = 25x$

$125x = 2000$

$\Rightarrow x = 16$

13. (B)

Let C.P. be ₹x and S.P. be ₹y.

Then, $3(y - x) = (2y - x) \Rightarrow y = 2x$

Profit = ₹$(y - x)$ = ₹$(2x - x)$ = ₹x

Profit % = $(x/x × 100)$ % = 100%

14. (B)

Let C.P. = ₹100. Then, Profit = ₹320,
 S.P. = ₹420

New C.P. = 125% of ₹100 = ₹125

New S.P. = ₹420

Profit = ₹$(420 - 125)$ = ₹295

Required percentage = $(295/420 × 100)$ % = $(1475/21)$ % = 70% (approximately).

15. (C)

C.P. of 6 toffees = ₹1

S.P. of 6 toffees = 120% of ` 1 = ₹6/5

For ₹6/5, toffees sold = 6.

For ₹1, toffees sold = $(6 × 5/6)$ = 5

16. (A)

Let C.P. be ₹x.

Then, $[(1920 - x)/x] × 100$

= $[(x - 1280)/x] × 100$

$\Rightarrow 1920 - x = x - 1280$

$\Rightarrow 2x = 3200$

$\Rightarrow x = 1600$

Required S.P. = 125% of ₹1600

= ₹$(125/100) × 1600$ = ₹2000

17. (C)

C.P. = ₹$[(100/122.5) × 392]$ = ₹320

Profit = ₹$(392 - 320)$ = ₹72.

18. (C)

S.P. = 85% of ` 1400 = ₹1190

19. (C)

Cost Price of 1 toy = ₹(375/12)

= ₹31.25

Selling Price of 1 toy = ₹33

So, Gain = ₹(33 - 31.25) = ₹1.75

Profit % = (1.75/31.25) × 100%

= 5.6%

20. (D)

Suppose, the number of articles bought
 = L.C.M. of 6 and 5 = 30

C.P. of 30 articles = ₹(5/6) × 30 = ₹25

S.P. of 30 articles = ₹(6/5) × 30 = ₹36

Gain % = (11/25 x 100) % = 44%

21. (A)

P.W. of ₹12,880 due 8 months hence

= ₹$[(12880 × 100)/ (100 + 18 × 8/12)]$

= ₹$(12880 × 100)/112$ = ₹11500

22. (A)

Required sum = P.W. of ₹702 due 6 months + P.W. of ₹702 due 1 year

hence

= $[(100 × 702)/(100 + 8 × 1/2)$

$+ (100 × 702)/(100 + 8 × 1)]$

= ₹$(675 + 650)$ = ₹1325

23. (A)

P.W. = $(100 × T.D.)/ R × T$

= $(100 × 168)/(14 × 2)$ = 600

∴ Sum = $(P.W. + T.D.)$ = ₹$(600 + 168)$

= ₹768

24. (C)

S.I. for 3 years = ₹$(12005 - 9800)$

= ₹2205

S.I. for 5 years = ₹$\frac{2205}{3} × 5$ = ₹3675

Principal = ₹$(9800 - 3675)$ = ₹6125

Hence, rate = $(100 × 3675)/(6125 × 5)$

= 12%

25. (B)

Let rate = R% and time = R years.

Then, $(1200 × R × R)/100 = 432$

$\Rightarrow 12R^2 = 432$

$\Rightarrow R^2 = 36$

$\Rightarrow R = 6$

26. (D)
Principal P = $ 10,000, Time Period T = 4 years and Rate of Interest = 2%
Putting these values in the simple interest formula,
I = (P × T × R)/100
 = 10,000 × 4 × 0.02
 = $ 800
Interest earned for the investment = $ 800

27. (B)
Principal = $ 15,000, Rate of Interest R = 10% = 0.10 and the Interest paid = I = $ 9,000. And T is to be found.
T = I/(PR)
 = 9000/(15,000 × 0.10)
 = 6 years.
The loan was given for 6 years.

28. (C)
Time
 = [100(Multiple number of principal − 1)] / Rate
 = [100(4 − 1)]/5 = 60 years

29. (B)
We may consider that ₹(1800 − 1650) gives interest of ₹30 at 4% per annum.
Therefore,
Time = (30 × 100)/ (150 × 4) = 5 years

30. (D)
Let us say Bobby invested ₹100.
Then, at the end of 'n' years he would have got back ₹400.
Therefore, the Simple Interest earned
 = 400 − 100 = ₹300.
Simple Interest = PRT/100
Substituting the values in the above equation of we get
$300 = (100 × n × 8)/100$
$\Rightarrow 8n = 300$
$\Rightarrow n = 37.5$ years $= 37$ years 6 months

31. (D)	32. (D)	33. (A)	34. (B)	35. (B)

31. (D)
100 cm is read as 102 cm.
$\therefore \quad A_1 = (100 × 100)$ cm^2 and $A_2 = (102 × 102)$ cm^2.
$(A_2 − A_1) = [(102)^2 − (100)^2]$
 $= (102 + 100) × (102 − 100)$
 $= 404$ cm^2
$\therefore$ Percentage error
 $= [404/(100 × 100) × 100]\% = 4.04\%$

32. (D)
Let original length $= x$
and original breadth $= y$
Decrease in area
$= xy − [(80/100)x × (90/100)y]$
$= (7/25)xy$
$\therefore$ Decrease % $= [(7/25)xy × 1/xy × 100]\%$
 $= 28\%$

34. (B)
Required money
= P.W. of ₹10028 due 9 months hence
$= ₹[(10028 × 100)/ (100 + 12 × 9/12)]$
= ₹9200

35. (B)
Let the sum be ₹100. Then,
S.I. for first 6 months
$$= ₹\left(\frac{100 \times 10 \times 1}{100 \times 2}\right) = ₹5$$
S.I. for last 6 months
$$= ₹\left(\frac{105 \times 10 \times 1}{100 \times 2}\right) = 5.25$$
So, amount at the end of 1 year
$= ₹(100 + 5 + 5.25) = ₹110.25$

Answer Key

1. (D)	2. (B)	3. (D)	4. (B)	5. (B)	6. (B)	7. (C)	8. (A)	9. (D)	10. (C)
11. (A)	12. (B)	13. (D)	14. (A)	15. (A)	16. (C)	17. (B)	18. (B)	19. (A)	20. (B)

1. (D)

Given, length of the rope = 68 m
and length of small piece

$$= 4\frac{1}{4}\,m = \frac{(4\times4)+1}{4}\,m = \frac{17}{4}\,m$$

∴ Number of pieces

$$= \frac{\text{Total length of rope}}{\text{Length of small piece}} = \frac{68}{17/4}$$

$$= \frac{68}{1}\times\frac{4}{17} \qquad \left[\because \text{reciprocal of } \frac{17}{4} = \frac{4}{17}\right]$$

$$= 4\times4 = 16$$

Hence, the number of pieces is 16.

2. (B)

Let the number be x.
We know that, greatest negativ integer is -1
According to the question,

$$x \div \left(\frac{-1}{2}\right) = -1$$

$$\Rightarrow \qquad x \times (-2) = -1$$

$$\Rightarrow \qquad x = \frac{-1}{-2}$$

$$\Rightarrow \qquad\qquad = \frac{1}{2}$$

Hence, the required number is $\frac{1}{2}$

3. (D)

$$8\times(x) = -10$$

$$\Rightarrow x = \frac{-10}{8} = \frac{-5}{4}$$

4. (B)

$$-\frac{15}{6} + x = -7$$

$$\Rightarrow x = -7 + \frac{15}{6} = \frac{-42+15}{6} = \frac{-27}{6} = \frac{-9}{2}$$

5. (B)

Here, $\dfrac{4}{5} + \dfrac{3}{7} = \dfrac{28+15}{35} = \dfrac{43}{15}$

Additive inverse of $\dfrac{43}{35} = \dfrac{-43}{35}$

6. (B)

$$2 - \frac{1}{2} - \frac{3}{4} = \frac{8-2-3}{4} = \frac{3}{4}$$

7. (C)

$$\frac{84}{288} = \frac{12\times7}{12\times24} = \frac{7}{24}$$

8. (A)

9. (D)

$$\frac{3}{13} \times x = -12 \Rightarrow x = \frac{-12\times13}{3} = -52$$

10. (C)

$$\frac{2}{3} < \frac{3}{4} < \frac{7}{8}$$

11. (A)

12. (B)

Cost of cloth per metre $= 98\dfrac{3}{4} \div 4\dfrac{1}{2}$

$$= \frac{395}{4} \div \frac{9}{2}$$

$$= \frac{395}{4} \times \frac{2}{9} = \frac{395}{18}$$

13. (D) $\left(\dfrac{3}{55} \times \dfrac{-33}{18}\right) - \left(\dfrac{39}{125} \times \dfrac{-15}{18}\right)$

$$= \frac{-1}{10} + \frac{3}{50} = \frac{-5+3}{50} = \frac{-2}{50}$$

$$= \frac{-1}{25}$$

14. (A)

$$\frac{2}{3} \div \frac{1}{3} - \frac{1}{2} \times \frac{1}{2}$$

$$= \frac{2}{3} \times \frac{3}{1} - \frac{1}{4} = 2 - \frac{1}{4} = \frac{8-1}{4} = \frac{7}{4}$$

Reciprocal of $\frac{7}{4} = \frac{4}{7}$

15. (A)

$$\frac{1}{\frac{-7}{9}} = \frac{-9}{7}$$

16. (C)

$$\frac{3}{2} + x = \frac{7}{4}$$

$$\Rightarrow x = \frac{7}{4} - \frac{3}{2} = \frac{7-6}{4} = \frac{1}{4}.$$

Other number = 4

17. (B)

$$\frac{121}{13} = \frac{x}{104}$$

$$\Rightarrow x = \frac{121 \times 104}{13} = 121 \times 8 = 968$$

18. (B)

$$\left(\frac{65}{12} + \frac{8}{3} \right) \div \left(\frac{65}{12} - \frac{8}{3} \right)$$

$$= \left(\frac{65+32}{12} \right) \div \left(\frac{65-32}{12} \right)$$

$$= \frac{97}{12} \div \frac{33}{12} = \frac{97}{12} \times \frac{12}{33} = \frac{97}{33}.$$

19. (A)

$$\frac{2}{3} + \frac{3}{4} = \frac{8+9}{12} = \frac{17}{12}$$

Multiplicative inverse of $\frac{17}{12} = \frac{12}{17}$

20. (B)

Cost of one article $= 87\frac{1}{2} \div 15$

$$= \frac{175}{2} \times \frac{1}{15} = \frac{35}{6}$$

HOTS (ACHIEVERS SECTION)

21. (A)	22. (B)	23. (C)	24. (A)	25. (A)

10. PRACTICAL GEOMETRY

Answer Key

1. (A)	2. (D)	3. (A)	4. (C)	5. (C)	6. (B)	7. (B)	8. (B)	9. (A)	10. (A)
11. (B)	12. (B)	13. (D)	14. (A)	15. (C)	16. (C)	17. (A)	18. (A)	19. (A)	20. (D)

1. (A)

If $\triangle ABC$ is right angle triangle then angle (hypo)2 = (side)² + (side)² (hypo)² = 12² + 5² (hypo)² = 144 + 25 (hypo)² = 169 (hypo) =√169 Hypo = 13 cm So AB = 13 cm

2. (D)

Pythagorean theorem, provides us with the relationship between the sides in a right triangle. A right triangle consists of two legs and a hypotenuse. The two legs meet at a 90° angle and the hypotenuse is the longest side of the right triangle and is the side opposite the right angle.

3. (A)

According to property Sum of the Lengths of Two Sides of a Triangle : The sum of the lengths of any two sides of a triangle is greater than the third side.

4. **(C)**

   Triangle with two sides of equal length are called isosceles triangle and the two angles opposite to sides of equal length is also equal.

5. **(C)**

   A triangle can have 3 altitudes drawn on all 3 sides only.

6. **(B)**

   A median of a triangle is a line segment joining a vertex to the midpoint of the opposite side.

7. **(B)**

   A median of a triangle is a line segment joining a vertex to the midpoint of the opposite side. A triangle therefore has three medians.

8. **(b)**

   The Pythagorean Theorem is the statement that the sum of the two small squares equals the big one. In algebraic terms, $a^2 + b^2 = c^2$ where c is the hypotenuse while a and b are the legs of the triangle.

9. **(A)**

   Pythagorean theorem In any right-angled triangle, the square of the length of hypotenuse is equal to the sum of the squares of the lengths of the other two sides.

10. **(A)**

    We know that, the sum of all the angles of a triangle is equal to 180°. So, sum of any two angles of a triangle should be less than 180°. 110°+ 40° = 150° i.e. less than 180°. 70° + 115° = 185° i.e. greater than 180°. 135° + 45°= 180° i.e. equal to 180°. 90° + 90° = 180° i.e. equal to 180°.

11. **(B)**

    Triangle can be constructed only if they satisfy the given condition. Sum of two sides > third side clearly, only option (B) satisfies the given condition. (2 + 3)cm > 4 cm i.e. 5 cm > 4 cm

12. **(B)**

    Square, triangle and circle are 2-D figures while sphere is the 3-D figure.

13. **(D)**

    The faces of a pyramid can be triangular and rectangular.

14. **(A)**

    If the three cubes are placed end to end that means length is increased. The new cuboid having dimensions 12 cm × 4 cm × 4 cm.

15. **(C)**

    The cone is the shape, that has only one vertex.

16. **(C)**

    To draw a parallel line to a given line l, we have to just copy the angle ∠AOL, so that

    ∠AOL = ∠AEM

    In this case AB act as a transverse and ∠AOL and ∠AEM are corresponding angles and they are equal if line l is parallel to line m

17. **(A)**

    The construction works by using the fact that a transverse line draws across two parallel lines create pairs of equal corresponding angles. It uses this in reverse by creating two equal corresponding angles, it can create the parallel lines.

18. **(A)**

    Steps of construction:
    Step 1. Draw a line segment AB=5cm
    Step 2. Assuming A as centre draw an arc of radius 3 cm
    Step 3. Now assuming B as centre draw an arc of 4 cm intersecting the previous arc at C.
    Step 4. Now join A to C and B to C.
    Hence, (A) will be correct.

19. **(A)**

    Correct sequence is
    Step 1: Draw a line segment of length DF = 8.6 cm.
    Step 2: Draw arcs of length 4 cm from D and 6.5 cm from F and mark the intersection point as E
    Step 3: Join D-E and F-E.
    So the sequence is 3-1-2

20. **(D)**

    Below are the correct steps.
    1. Draw a line segment which is sufficiently long using ruler.

2. Locate points A and B on it such that AB=5.5 cm

3. At A construct a line segment AE, sufficiently large, such that $\angle BAC = 70°$, use protractor to measure 70°.

4. With A as centre and radius 6.5 cm draw the line cutting AE at C, join BC then ABC is the required triangle.

Hence, (D) will be correct answer.

<table>
<tr><th colspan="5">HOTS (ACHIEVERS SECTION)</th></tr>
<tr><td>21. (A)</td><td>22. (C)</td><td>23. (A)</td><td>24. (D)</td><td>25. (B)</td></tr>
</table>

22. (C)
Steps of Construction:
i. Draw a line segment PQ = 10cm.
ii. At P, draw a ray making an angle of 30°.
iii. At Q, draw another ray making an angle of 60° which intersects the first ray at R.

ΔPQR is the required triangle.

Hence, (C) will be correct answer.

24. (D)
Steps of Construction:
i. Draw a line segment PQ = 10cm.
ii. At P, draw a ray making an angle of 30°.

iii. At Q, draw another ray making an angle of 60° which intersects the first ray at R.

ΔPQR is the required triangle.

Hence, (D) will be correct answer.

25. (B)
Steps of Construction:
i. Draw a line segment PQ = 10cm.
ii. At P, draw a ray making an angle of 30°.
iii. At Q, draw another ray making an angle of 60° which intersects the first ray at R.

Δ PQR is the required triangle.

Hence, (B) will be the correct answer.

11. ELEMENTARY MENSURATION

<table>
<tr><th colspan="10">Answer Key</th></tr>
<tr><td>1. (C)</td><td>2. (D)</td><td>3. (C)</td><td>4. (B)</td><td>5. (A)</td><td>6. (D)</td><td>7. (B)</td><td>8. (D)</td><td>9. (D)</td><td>10. (C)</td></tr>
<tr><td>11. (C)</td><td>12. (D)</td><td>13. (A)</td><td>14. (D)</td><td>15. (C)</td><td>16. (A)</td><td>17. (B)</td><td>18. (D)</td><td>19. (D)</td><td>20. (A)</td></tr>
<tr><td>21. (C)</td><td>22. (A)</td><td>23. (B)</td><td>24. (B)</td><td>25. (B)</td><td></td><td></td><td></td><td></td><td></td></tr>
</table>

1. (C)

Other side $= \sqrt{(7.5)^2 - (4.5)^2}$ ft

$= \sqrt{\dfrac{144}{4}} = 6\,\text{ft}$

∴ Area of closet = (6 × 4.5) sq. ft = 27 sq. ft.

2. (D)

Let original length = x
and original breadth = y
Decrease in area
$= xy - [(80/100)x × (90/100)y]$

$= (7/25)xy$

∴ Decrease % $= [(7/25)xy × 1/xy × 100]\%$
$= 28\%$

3. (C)

Let the side of the square (ABCD) be x metres.

Then, AB + BC = $2x$ metres.

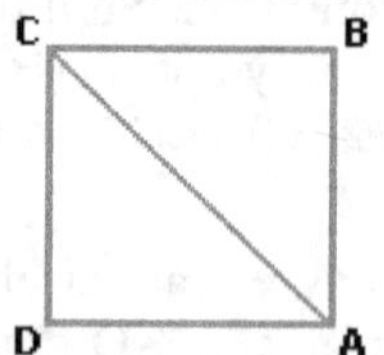

$AC = \sqrt{2}x = (1.41x)$ m.

Saving on $2x$ metres $= (0.59x)$ m.

Saving % $= (0.59x/2x) \times 100\%$

   $= 30\%$ (approx)

4. **(B)**

If l and b are length and breadth then

$\sqrt{l^2 + b^2} = \sqrt{41}$

Also, $lb = 20$

$(l + b)^2 = (l^2 + b^2) + 2lb = 41 + 40 = 81$

$\Rightarrow (l + b) = 9$

∴ Perimeter $= 2(l + b) = 2 \times 9 = 18$ cm.

5. **(A)**

Length of largest tile

$=$ H.C.F. of 1517 cm and 902 cm $= 41$ cm.

Area of each tile $= (41 \times 41)$ cm^2.

∴ Required number of tiles

   $= (1517 \times 902)/(41 \times 41) = 814$

6. **(D)**

We have: $(l - b) = 23$ and $2(l + b) = 206$ or $(l + b) = 103$.

where, $l =$ length, $b =$ breath

Solving these two equations, we get:

   $l = 63$ and $b = 40$.

∴ Area $= (l \times b) = (63 \times 40)$ m^2

   $= 2520$ m2.

7. **(B)**

Let original length $= x$

and original breadth $= y$

Original area $= xy$.

New length $= x/2$

New breadth $= 3y$.

New area $= (x/2 \times 3y) = (3/2)xy$

∴ Increase % $= (1/2)xy \times (1/xy) \times 100\%$

   $= 50\%$

8. **(D)**

Let breadth $= x$ metres.

Then, length $= (x + 20)$ metres.

Perimeter $= (5300/26.50)$ m $= 200$ m

∴ $2[(x + 20) + x] = 200$

$\Rightarrow 2x + 20 = 100$

$\Rightarrow 2x = 80$

$\Rightarrow x = 40$

Hence, length $= x + 20 = 60$ m.

9. **(D)**

We have: $l = 20$ ft and $lb = 680$ sq. ft.

So, $b = 34$ ft.

∴ Length of fencing $= (l + 2b)$

   $= (20 + 68)$ ft $= 88$ ft.

10. **(C)**

Area to be plastered

$= [2(l + b) \times h] + (l \times b)$

$= \{[2(25 + 12) \times 6] + (25 \times 12)\}$ m^2

$= (444 + 300)$ m^2

$= 744$ m^2.

∴ Cost of plastering $= ₹(744 \times 75/100)$

   $= ₹558$

11. **(C)**

Area $= 1600$ m^2.

I. Side $= 1600$ m $= 40$ m. So, perimeter

   $= (40 \times 4)$ m $= 160$ m.

∴ I alone gives the answer.

II. Perimeter $=$ Total cost $= 3200$ m

   $= 160$ m

Cost per metre $= 20$

∴ II alone gives the answer.

∴ Correct answer is (C).

12. **(D)**

Given: Area of rectangle

$=$ Area of a right-angle triangle.

$\Rightarrow l \times b = \frac{1}{2} \times B \times H$

I gives, $B = 40$ cm.

II gives, $H = 50$ cm.

Thus, to find l, we need b also, which is not given.

∴ Given data is not sufficient to give the answer.

∴ Correct answer is (D).

13. **(A)**

I. $A = 20 \times B \Rightarrow \frac{1}{2} \times B \times H = 20 \times B \Rightarrow H = 40$.

∴ I alone gives the answer.

II gives the perimeter of the triangle $= 40$ cm.

This does not give the height of the triangle.

∴ Correct answer is (A).

14. **(D)**
   I gives, 2 πR = 44
   II gives, H = 12.
   ∴ A = 2 πRH = (4 × 12)
   Cost of painting = ` (44 × 12 × 20)
   Thus, I and II together give the answer.
   ∴ Correct answer is (D).

15. **(C)**
   I. Material cost = ₹2.50 per m²
   II. Labour cost = ₹3500
   III. Total cost = ₹14,500
   Let the area be A sq. metres.
   ∴ Material cost = ₹ (14500 – 3500)
   $\qquad\qquad$ = ₹11,000
   ∴ 5A/2 = 11000
   A = (11000 × 2)/5 = 4400 m²
   Thus, all I, II and III are needed to get the answer.
   ∴ Correct answer is (C).

16. **(A)**
   From II, base : height = 5 : 12
   Let base = 5x and height = 12x
   Then, hypotenuse
   $$= \sqrt{(5x)^2 + (12x)^2} = 13x$$
   From I, perimeter of the triangle = 30 cm.
   ∴ 5x + 12x + 13x = 30 ⇒ x = 1
   So, base = 5x = 5 cm, height = 12x = 12 cm.
   ∴ Area = (1/2 × 5 × 12) = 30 cm²
   Thus, I and II together give the answer.
   Clearly III is redundant, since the breadth of the rectangle is not given.
   ∴ Correct answer is (A).

17. **(B)**
   I. 2(l + b) = 110 ⇒ l + b = 55
   II. l = (b + 5) $\qquad$ ⇒ l – b = 5
   III. l/b = 6/5 $\qquad$ ⇒ 5l – 6b = 0
   These are three equations in l and b. We may solve them pair-wise.
   ∴ Any two of the three will give the answer.
   ∴ Correct answer is (B).

18. **(D)**
   From I and II, we can find the length and breadth of the rectangle and therefore the area can be obtained.
   So, III is redundant.
   Also, from II and III, we can find the length and breadth and therefore the area can be obtained.
   So, I is redundant.
   ∴ Correct answer is "II and either I or III".

19. **(D)**
   From II, let l = 4x, b = 6x; and h = 5x.
   Then, area of the hall = (24x^2) m².
   From I. Area of the hall = 24 m².
   From II and I, we get 24x^2 = 24 ⇒ x = 1.
   ∴ l = 4 m, b = 6 and h = 5 m.
   Thus, the area of two adjacent walls
   = [(l × h) + (b × h)] m² can be found out and so the cost of painting two adjacent walls may be found out.
   Thus, III is redundant.
   ∴ Correct answer is (D).

20. **(A)**
   By the formula:
   Required area = π (14/2)² = 22/7 × 7²
   $\qquad\qquad\qquad$ = 154 cm²

21. **(C)**
   Area of quadrilateral = $\dfrac{1}{2}$ × any diagonal × (sum of perpendiculars drawn on diagonal from two vertices)
   $$= \frac{1}{2} \times D \times (P_1 + P_2)$$
   $$= \frac{1}{2} \times 23 \times (17 + 7) = 12 \times 23$$
   $$= 276 \text{ cm}^2$$

22. **(A)**
   Circumference of the circle = 2πr
   ∴ $r = \dfrac{50}{\pi}$
   ∴ Side of the inscribed square
   $$= \sqrt{2}r = \sqrt{2} \times \frac{50}{\pi}$$

23. **(B)**

% increase in its area
$= 2 × 5 + 5^2/100$
$= 10 + 0.25 = 10.25\%$

24. (B)
Required percentage increase
$= 2 × 2 + 2^2/100$
$= 4 + 0.04$
$= 4.04\%$

25. (B)
Diameter is rarely used as the measuring side of a circle. Thus % increase in circumference = 12%

HOTS (ACHIEVERS SECTION)

26. (C)	27. (D)	28. (A)	29. (D)	30. (C)

26. (C)
Area = 1600 m².
I. Side = $\sqrt{1600}$ m = 40 m. So, perimeter
= (40 × 4) m = 160 m.
∴ I alone gives the answer.
II. Perimeter = Total cost = 3200 m
= 160 m
Cost per metre = 20
∴ II alone gives the answer.
∴ Correct answer is (C).

27. (D)
Given: Area of rectangle
= Area of a right-angle triangle.
$⇒ l × b = $ ½ × B × H
I gives, B = 40 cm.
II gives, H = 50 cm.
Thus, to find l, we need b also, which is not given.
∴ Given data is not sufficient to give the answer.
∴ Correct answer is (D).

28. (A)
I. A = 20 x B $⇒$ ½ x B x H = 20 x B $⇒$ H = 40.
∴ I alone gives the answer.

II gives the perimeter of the triangle = 40 cm.
This does not give the height of the triangle.
∴ Correct answer is (A).

29. (D)
I gives, 2 πR = 44
II gives, H = 12.
∴ A = 2 πRH = (4 × 12)
Cost of painting = ₹ (44 × 12 × 20)
Thus, I and II together give the answer.
∴ Correct answer is (D).

30. (C)
I. Material cost = ₹2.50 per m²
II. Labour cost = ₹3500
III. Total cost = ₹14,500
Let the area be A sq. metres.
∴ Material cost = ₹ (14500 – 3500)
= ₹11,000
∴ 5A/2 = 11000
A = (11000 × 2)/5 = 4400 m²
Thus, all I, II and III are needed to get the answer.
∴ Correct answer is (C).

Answer Key

1. (C)	2. (A)	3. (A)	4. (B)	5. (D)	6. (B)	7. (A)	8. (B)	9. (B)	10. (A)
11. (C)	12. (D)	13. (B)	14. (A)	15. (B)	16. (A)	17. (B)	18. (A)	19. (C)	20. (A)
21. (A)	22. (B)	23. (C)	24. (D)	25. (A)					

1. **(C)**

$$(-3m^2np) \times \left(\frac{1}{3}nm^3p^2\right) \times \left(\frac{2}{3}m^2n^2p^2\right)$$

$$= -3 \times \frac{1}{3} \times \frac{2}{3} \, m^2 \times m^3 \times m^2 \times n \times n \times n^2 \times p \times p^2 \times p^2$$

$$= -\frac{2}{3}m^7n^4p^5$$

2. **(A)**

$$(-xyz^2)(-2yx^2z)\left(\frac{1}{2}x^3yz\right)$$

$$= 2 \times \frac{1}{2}x \times x^2 \times x^3 \times y \times y \times y \times z^2z \times z$$

$$= x^6y^3z^4$$

3. **(A)**

$$5 - (3x + 2y) - 3(x - y) + 7x + y$$
$$= 5 - 3x - 2y - 3x + 3y + 7x + y$$
$$= 5 + x + 2y$$

4. **(B)**

Sum $= (3x^2 + 5y^2) + (x^2 - 4y^2) = 4x^2 + y^2$

Difference $= (2x^2 + 3y^2) - (x^2 - y^2)$
$$= 2x^2 + 3y^2 - x^2 + y^2$$
$$= x^2 + 4y^2$$

Product $= (4x^2 + y^2)(x^2 + 4y^2)$
$$= 4x^4 + 16x^2y^2 + x^2y^2 + 4y^4$$
$$= 4x^4 + 17x^2y^2 + 4y^4$$

5. **(D)**

$$(2.3\,a^5b^2) \times (1.2a^2b^2)$$
$$= 2.3 \times 1.2\,a^7b^4$$
$$= 2.76 \times (1)^7 \times (0.5)^4$$
$$= 2.76 \times 0.25 \times 0.25 = 0.1725$$

6. **(B)**

$$(2.6\,m^2n) \times (5\,mn^2)$$

$$= 2.6 \times 5 \times m^2 \times m \times n \times n^2$$

$$= 13 \times \left(\frac{1}{2}\right)^3 \times \left(\frac{1}{3}\right)^3$$

$$= 13 \times \frac{1}{8} \times \frac{1}{27} = \frac{13}{216}$$

7. **(A)**

$$(ab^2c)(-a^2bc^2)(-abc^3)(-a^2bc)$$
$$= -a \times a^2 \times a \times a^2 \times b^2 \times b \times b \times b \times c$$
$$\times c^2 \times c^3 \times c$$
$$= -a^6b^5c^7$$

8. **(B)**

$$\left(3x - \frac{4}{5}xy^2\right)\left(\frac{1}{3}xy\right)$$

$$= 3x \times \frac{1}{3}xy - \frac{4}{5}xy^2 \times \frac{1}{3}xy$$

$$= x^2y - \frac{4}{15}x^2y^3$$

9. **(B)**

$$3s(s^2 - st)$$
$$= 3s^3 - 3s^2t$$
$$= 3(2)^3 - 3(2)^2 \times 5$$
$$= 3 \times 8 - 3 \times 4 \times 5$$
$$= 24 - 60 = -36$$

10. **(A)**

$$a(b - c) + b(c - a) + c(a - b)$$
$$= ab - ac + bc - ab + ac - bc$$
$$= 0$$

11. **(C)**

$$a(b - 2c) + 2b(c - 2a) + c(3a - 2b)$$
$$= ab - 2ac + 2bc - 4ab + 3ac - 2bc$$
$$= ac - 3ab$$

12. (D)
$(-3x^2y^2z^2)(-5xy^2z)$
$= (-3)(-5)x^3y^4z^3$
$= 15x^3y^4z^3$

13. (B)
$a(b - c) - b(c - 2a) - c(2a - b)$
$= ab - ac - bc + 2ab - 2ac + bc$
$= 3ab - 3ac = 3(ab - ac) = 3a(b - c)$

14. (A)
$$\left(x^4 - \frac{1}{x^4}\right)\left(x + \frac{1}{x}\right)$$

$$= x^5 + x^4 \times \frac{1}{x} - \frac{1}{x^4} \times x - \frac{1}{x^5}$$

$$= x^5 + x^3 - \frac{1}{x^3} - \frac{1}{x^5}$$

15. (B)
$(x^3 + y^3)(x^2 - y^2)$
$= (x^3)(x^2) - (x^3)(y^2) + (y^3)(x^2) - (y^3)(y^2)$
$= x^5 - x^3y^2 + x^2y^3 - y^5$

16. (A)
$2x^2 - 3xy - y^2 - yz - (x^2 - xy + y^2 + yz)$
$= 2x^2 - 3xy - y^2 - yz - x^2 + xy - y^2 - yz$
$= x^2 - 2xy - 2y^2 - 2yz$

17. (B)
Sum $= -5x^2 + 7xy + 2y^2 + x^2 - 3xy - y^2$
$= -4x^2 + 4xy + y^2$
Then $-7 - (-4x^2 + 4xy + y^2)$
$= -7 + 4x^2 - 4xy - y^2)$

18. (A)
$(0.8m - 0.7n)(1.5n - 1.7m)$
$= (0.8m)(1.5n) + (0.7n)(1.7m) - (0.7n)$
$(1.5n) - (0.8m)(1.7m)$
$= 1.2mn + 1.19mn - 1.05n^2 - 1.36m^2$
$= 2.39mn - 1.05n^2 - 1.36m^2$

19. (C)
$0.3x^2 - 3xy + 0.8y^2 + 4x^2 - 2y^2 + 0.7xy$
$= (4 + 0.3)x^2 + (0.7 - 3)xy + (0.8 - 2)y^2$
$= 4.3x^2 - 2.3xy - 1.2y^2$

20. (A)
$(7x^2 - x + 11)(x^2 - 3)$
$= 7x^4 - 21x^2 - x^3 + 3x + 11x^2 - 33$
$= 7x^4 - x^3 - 10x^2 + 3x - 33$

21. (A)
$1.5a(10a^2b - 100ab^2)$
$= 15a^3b - 150a^2b^2$

22. (B)
$7x^2 - [x^2 - 3x - \{x + y\}] - (5x - 3y + 3)$
$= 7x^2 - x^2 + 3x + x + y - 5x + 3y - 3$
$= 6x^2 - x + 4y - 3$

23. (C)
$x(x + 4) + 3x(2x^2 - 3) + 4x^2 + 5$
$= x^2 + 4x + 6x^3 - 9x + 4x^2 + 5$
$= 6x^3 + 5x^2 - 5x + 5$

24. (D)
$4mn(m - n) - 6m^2(n - n^2) - 3n^2(2m^2 - m)$
$= 4m^2n - 4mn^2 - 6m^2n + 6m^2n^2$
$- 6n^2m^2 + 3n^2m$
$= -2m^2n - n^2m = -mn(2m + n)$

25. (A)
$a^2b(a - b^2) - ab^2(3ab - a^2) - a^3b(1 - 2b)$
$= a^3b - a^2b^3 - 3a^2b^3 + a^3b^2 - a^3b + 2a^3b^2$
$= 3a^3b^2 - 4a^2b^3$

HOTS (ACHIEVERS SECTION)

26. (A)	27. (A)	28. (A)	29. (B)	30. (C)

13. EXPONENTS AND POWERS

Answer Key

1. (B)	2. (B)	3. (C)	4. (A)	5. (C)	6. (D)	7. (D)	8. (A)	9. (B)	10. (D)
11. (C)	12. (A)	13. (C)	14. (C)	15. (B)	16. (C)	17. (D)	18. (C)	19. (B)	20. (C)

HINTS AND SOLUTIONS

1. **(B)**
Given $(25)^{7.5} \times (5)^{2.5} \div (125)^{1.5} = 5^x$
Then, $(5^2)^{7.5} \times (5)^{2.5} \div (5^3)^{1.5} = 5^x$
$\Rightarrow 5^{(2 \times 7.5)} \times 5^{2.5} \div 5^{(3 \times 1.5)} = 5^x$
$\Rightarrow 5^{15} \times 5^{2.5} \div 5^{4.5} = 5^x$
$\Rightarrow 5^x = 5^{(15 + 2.5 - 4.5)}$
$\Rightarrow 5^x = 5^{13}$
$\Rightarrow x = 13$

2. **(B)**
$(0.04)^{-1.5} = (4/100)^{-1.5} = (1/25)^{-3/2}$
$\quad = (25)^{(3/2)}$
$\quad = (5^2)^{(3/2)}$
$\quad = (5)^{2 \times (3/2)}$
$\quad = 5^3$
$\quad = 125$

3. **(C)**
$3^{x-y} = 27 = 3^3 \Rightarrow x - y = 3 \;....(i)$
$3^{x+y} = 243 = 3^5 \Rightarrow x + y = 5 \;.... (ii)$
On solving (i) and (ii), we get $x = 4$.

4. **(A)**
$5^a = 3125 \Leftrightarrow 5^a = 5^5$
$\Rightarrow a = 5$
$\therefore 5^{(a-3)} = 5^{(5-3)} = 5^2 = 25$

5. **(C)**
$x^z = y^2 \Rightarrow 10^{(0.48z)} = 10^{(2 \times 0.70)} = 10^{1.40}$
$\Rightarrow 0.48z = 1.40$
$\Rightarrow z = 140/48 = 35/12 = 2.9$ (approx.)

6. **(D)**
Let $(17)^{3.5} \times (17)^x = 17^8$
Then, $(17)^{3.5 + x} = 17^8$
$\therefore 3.5 + x = 8$
$\Rightarrow x = (8 - 3.5)$
$\Rightarrow x = 4.5$

7. **(D)**
$$\sqrt{300} = \sqrt{10 \times 10 \times 3} = 10\sqrt{3}$$
$$= 10 \times 1.732 = 17.32$$

8. **(A)**
$$\sqrt{75} + \sqrt{147} =$$
$$\sqrt{5 \times 5 \times 3} + \sqrt{7 \times 7 \times 3}$$
$$= 5\sqrt{3} + 7\sqrt{3} = 12\sqrt{3}$$
$$= 12 \times 1.732 = 20.7846$$

9. **(B)**
$$\sqrt{80} + 3\sqrt{245} - \sqrt{125}$$
$$= \sqrt{4 \times 4 \times 5} + 3\sqrt{7 \times 7 \times 5} - \sqrt{5 \times 5 \times 5}$$
$$= 4\sqrt{5} + 21\sqrt{5} - 5\sqrt{5}$$
$$= 20\sqrt{5} = 44.7214$$

10. **(D)**
$$\sqrt{242} \div \sqrt{72} = \frac{\sqrt{121 \times 2}}{\sqrt{36 \times 2}}$$
$$= \frac{11\sqrt{2}}{6\sqrt{2}}$$
$$= \frac{11}{6} = 1\frac{5}{6}$$

11. **(C)**
$(18a^8b^6) \div (3a^2b^2) = 18/3 \times a^{8-2} \times b^{6-2}$
$\qquad\qquad = 6a^6b^4$

12. **(A)**
$56 - 45 - \sqrt{?} = \sqrt{36}$
$\Rightarrow 11 - \sqrt{36} = \sqrt{?}$
$\Rightarrow 11 - 6 = \sqrt{?}$
$\therefore ? = 25$

13. (C)

$$?^2 = \frac{4}{25}$$

$$? = \sqrt{\frac{4}{25}} = \frac{2}{5}$$

14. (C)

$$\Rightarrow \sqrt{210\frac{1}{4}} = \sqrt{\frac{841}{4}} = \sqrt{\frac{29 \times 29}{4}} = \frac{29}{2} = 14\frac{1}{2}$$

15. (B)

$(0.003)^3 = 0.003 \times 0.003 \times 0.003$

$\qquad = 0.000000027$

16. (C)

We can wirte the given expression as

$$\frac{10^{22}}{10^{20}} + \frac{10^{20}}{10^{20}} = 10^{20-20} + 1$$

$$\left[\because \frac{a^m}{a^n} = a^{m-n}, m > n \right]$$

$= 10^2 + 1 = 10 \times 10 + 1 = 100 + 1 = 101$

17. (D)

A number in standard form is written as $a \times 10^k$, where a is a terminating decimal such that $1 \le a \le 10$ and k is any integer.

So, $12345 = 1.2345 \times 10^4$

18. (C)

Given

$$2^{1998} - 2^{1997} - 2^{1996} + 2^{1995} = k.2^{1995}$$

$$\Rightarrow 2^{1995+3} - 2^{1995+2} - 2^{1995+1} + 2^{1995} \times 1$$
$$= k.2^{1995}$$

$$\Rightarrow 2^{1995}[2^3 - 2^2 - 2^1 + 1] = k.2^{1995}$$

$[\because am+n = am \times an]$

$$\Rightarrow 21995[8 - 4 - 2 + 1] = k.2^{1995}$$

$$\Rightarrow 3 = 3 = \frac{k.2^{1995}}{2^{1995}}$$

$\Rightarrow 3 = k$ or $k = 3$

So the value of k is 3.

19. (B)

$2^0 \times 3^0 \times 4^0 = 1 \times 1 \times 1 \quad [\because a^0 = 1]$

$= 1$

Hence, option (b) is the answer.

20. (C)

We know that, $\left(\dfrac{p}{q} \right)^m = \dfrac{p^m}{q^m}$

So, $\left(\dfrac{-5}{4} \right)^4 = \dfrac{\left(-5^4 \right)}{(4)^4}$ or $\left(\dfrac{-5}{4} \right)^4 = \dfrac{(5)^4}{(-4)^4}$

$$\left(\frac{-5}{4} \right)^4 = \left(\frac{-5}{4} \right) \times \left(\frac{-5}{4} \right) \times \left(\frac{-5}{4} \right) \times \left(\frac{-5}{4} \right)$$

Hence, option (C) is not equal to the given term.

<table>
<tr><td colspan="5" align="center">HOTS (ACHIEVERS SECTION)</td></tr>
<tr><td>21. (C)</td><td>22. (D)</td><td>23. (A)</td><td>24. (C)</td><td>25. (B)</td></tr>
</table>

14. SYMMETRY

Answer Key

1. (D)	2. (C)	3. (C)	4. (D)	5. (B)	6. (C)	7. (C)	8. (A)	9. (C)	10. (B)
11. (B)	12. (B)	13. (B)	14. (C)	15. (C)	16. (A)	17. (A)	18. (D)	19. (A)	20. (D)

1. (D)

A regular pentagon has 5 sides so the number of lines of symmetry in regular pentagon are equal to the number of sides where each one goes form a vertex to the midpoint of the opposite side.

2. (C)

The two lines passes through the corners of the rhombus and divide the rhombus in two equal parts.

3. (C)
A triangle has two equal side has exactly one axis of symmetry which goes through the mid point of the base and divide the triangle in two equal parts.

5. (B)
The windmill of four blades has a rotational symmetry of order 4.
$\therefore\ 2K = 4 \Rightarrow K = 2$

6. (C)
An equilateral triangle has 3 lines of symmetry.

9. (C)
P has no line of symmetry.

HOTS (ACHIEVERS SECTION)

21. (B)	22. (B)	23. (C)	24. (D)	25. (B)

21. (B)
Reflection symmetry occurs when a line is used to split an object or shape in halves so that each half reflect the other half. The image of V has reflection line of symmetry about vertical mirror that mean it split the image of V in two equal parts and one half would reflect the other half.

22. (B)
The one line of symmetry divides a rectangle in half horizontally and the other line divides the rectangle in half vertically.

23. (C)
Square has four equal sides that means the two lines passes through each diagonal and the other two lines cross horizontally and vertically through the middle of the square, these four lines of symmetry divides the square in two equal parts

24. (D)
As the regular hexagon has 6 equal sides, so there are 6 lines of symmetry to divides the regular hexagon in two equal parts.

15. VISUALIZING SOLID SHAPES

Answer Key

1. (B)	2. (B)	3. (C)	4. (A)	5. (B)	6. (B)	7. (B)	8. (C)	9. (C)	10. (C)
11. (C)	12. (D)	13. (C)	14. (D)	15. (C)	16. (D)	17. (B)	18. (C)	19. (D)	20. (B)

1. (B)
Volume of water displaced
$= (3 \times 2 \times 0.01)$ m³
$= 0.06$ m³
$\therefore$ Mass of man = Volume of water displaced × Density of water
$= (0.06 \times 1000)$ kg
$= 60$ kg

2. (B)
Total volume of water displaced
$= (4 \times 50)$ m³ $= 200$ m³
$\therefore$ Rise in water level $= [200/(40 \times 20)]$ m
$= 0.25$ m $= 25$ cm

3. (C)
$l = 10$ m
$h = 8$ m

So, $r = \sqrt{l^2 - h^2} = \sqrt{10^2 - 8^2} = 6$ m

$\therefore$ Curved surface area = πrl

$= (\pi \times 6 \times 10)$ m$^2 = 60 \, \pi$ m^2

4. **(A)**

Area of the wet surface

$= [2(lb + bh + lh) - lb]$

$= 2(bh + lh) + lb$

$= [2 (4 \times 1.25 + 6 \times 1.25) + 6 \times 4]$ m^2

$= 49$ m^2

5. **(B)**

Clearly, $l = (48 - 16)$m $= 32$ m,

$b = (36 - 16)$m $= 20$ m

$h = 8$ m.

$\therefore$ Volume of the box $= (32 \times 20 \times 8)$ m^3

$\qquad\qquad = 5120$ m^3

6. **(B)**

$(\pi r^2 h)/ (2\pi rh) = 924/264$

$r = [(924 /264) \times 2] = 7$ m

and, $2\pi rh = 264$

$h = (264 \times 7/22 \times 1/2 \times 1/7) = 6$ m

$\therefore$ Required ratio = $2r/h = 14/6 = 7 : 3$

7. **(B)**

Let the thickness of the base be x cm.

Then, $[(330 - 10) \times (260 - 10) \times (110 - x)]$

$= 8000 \times 1000$

$\Rightarrow 320 \times 250 \times (110 - x) = 8000 \times 1000$

$\Rightarrow (110 - x) = (8000 \times 1000)/ (320 \times 250)$

$\qquad = 100$

$x = 10$ cm $= 1$ dm

8. **(C)**

$h = 14$ cm, $r = 7$ cm.

So, $l = \sqrt{7^2 + 14^2} = \sqrt{245} = 7\sqrt{5}$ cm.

$\therefore$ Total surface area = $\pi rl + \pi r^2$

$= (22/7 \times 7 \times 7\sqrt{5} + 22/7 \times 7^2)$ cm^2

$= [154(\sqrt{5} + 1)]$ cm$^2 = (154 \times 3.236)$ cm^2

$= 498.35$ cm^2

9. **(C)**

Volume of the large cube $= (3^3 + 4^3 + 5^3)$

$\qquad\qquad\qquad = 216$ cm^3

Let the edge of the large cube be a.

So, $a^3 = 216 \quad \Rightarrow \quad a = 6$ cm

$\therefore$ Required ratio

$= [6 \times (3^2 + 4^2 + 5^2)]/ (6 \times 6^2)$

$= 50/36 = 25 : 18$

10. **(C)**

Number of bricks $= \dfrac{\text{Volume of the wall}}{\text{Volume of 1 brick}}$

$= \dfrac{(800 \times 600 \times 22.5)}{(25 \times 11.25 \times 6)}$

$= 6400$

11. **(C)**

Given, height $= 32$ m

From I, the area of the base $= 154$ m^2

$\therefore$ Volume = (Area of the base $\times$ Height)

$\qquad\qquad = (154 \times 32)$ m^3

Thus, I alone can give the answer.

From II, the radius of the base $= 7$ m

$\therefore$ Volume $= \pi r^2 h = (22/7 \times 7 \times 7 \times 32)$ m^3

$= 4928$ m^3

Thus, II alone can give the answer.

$\therefore$ Correct answer is (C).

12. **(D)**

From I, any two of l, b, h are equal.

From II, lbh = 64.

From I and II, the values of l, b, h may be
(1, 1, 64), (2, 2, 16), (4, 4, 4).

Thus, the block may be a cube or cuboid.

$\therefore$ Correct answer is (D).

13. **(C)**

From I, h = 28 m and r = 14.

$\therefore$ Capacity = $\pi r^2 h$, which can be obtained.

Thus, I alone can give the answer.

From II, $\pi r^2 = 616$ m^2 and h = 28 m

$\therefore$ Capacity = $(\pi r^2 \times h) = (616 \times 28)$ m^3

Thus, II alone can give the answer.

$\therefore$ Correct answer is (C).

14. **(D)**

II gives the value of r.

But, in I, the breadth of rectangle is not given.

So, we cannot find the surface area of the cone.

Hence, the height of the cone cannot be
determined.

$\therefore$ Correct answer is (D).

15. **(C)**

Let each edge be a metre. Then,

I. $a^2 = 64$

$a = 8$ m

Volume = $(8 \times 8 \times 8)$ m³ = 512 m³

Thus, I alone can give the answer.

II. $a = 8$ m

Volume = $(8 \times 8 \times 8)$ m³ = 512 m³

Thus, II alone can give the answer.

∴ Correct answer is (C).

16. (D)

Capacity = $\pi r^2 h$

From I, $\pi r^2 = 61600$. This gives r.

From II, h = 1.5 r

Thus, I and II give the answer.

Again, III gives 2 πr = 880. This gives r.

So, II and III also give the answer.

∴ Correct answer is (D).

17. (B)

Part filled by (A + B + C) in 3 minutes = 3 (1/30 + 1/20 + 1/10) = (3 × 11/60) = 11/20

Part filled by C in 3 minutes = 3/10

∴ Required ratio = (3/10 × 20/11) = 6/11

18. (C)

Net part filled in 1 hour (1/5 + 1/6 − 1/12)

= 17/60

∴ The tank will be full in 60/17 hours i.e.,

$3\dfrac{9}{17}$ hours

19. (D)

Work done by the leak in 1 hour

= (1/2 − 3/7) = 1/14

∴ Leak will empty the tank in 14 hrs.

20. (B)

Let B be turned off after x minutes. Then,

Part filled by (A + B) in x min. + Part filled by A in (30 − x) min. = 1.

x(2/75 + 1/45) + (30 − x)2/75 = 1

⇒ 11x/225 + (60 − 2x)/75 = 1

⇒ 11x + 180 − 6x = 225

⇒ $x = 9$

<table>
<tr><td colspan="5" align="center">HOTS (ACHIEVERS SECTION)</td></tr>
<tr><td>21. (D)</td><td>22. (C)</td><td>23. (D)</td><td>24. (D)</td><td>25. (B)</td></tr>
</table>

21. (D)

From I, any two of l, b, h are equal.

From II, $lbh = 64$.

From I and II, the values of l, b, h may be (1, 1, 64), (2, 2, 16), (4, 4, 4).

Thus, the block may be a cube or cuboid.

∴ Correct answer is (D).

22. (C)

From I, $h = 28$ m and $r = 14$.

∴ Capacity = $\pi r^2 h$, which can be obtained.

Thus, I alone can give the answer.

From II, $\pi r^2 = 616$ m² and $h = 28$ m

∴ Capacity = $(\pi r^2 \times h) = (616 \times 28)$ m³

Thus, II alone can give the answer.

∴ Correct answer is (C).

23. (D)

I. Time taken to fill the cistern without leak = 9 hours.

Part of cistern filled without leak in 1 hour = 1/9

II. Time taken to fill the cistern in presence of leak = 10 hours.

Net filling in 1 hour = 1/10

Work done by leak in 1 hour = (1/9 − 1/10) = 1/90

∴ Leak will empty the full cistern in 90 hours.

Clearly, both I and II are necessary to answer the question.

∴ Correct answer is (D).

24. (D)

I. A's 1 minute's filling work = 1/16

II. B's 1 minute's filling work = 1/8

(A + B)'s 1 minute's emptying work = (1/8 − 1/16) = 1/16

∴ Tank will be emptied in 16 minutes.

Thus, both I and II are necessary to answer the question.

∴ Correct answer is (D).

25. **(B)**

II. Part of the tank filled by A in 1 hour = 1/4

III. Part of the tank filled by B in 1 hour = 1/6

(A + B)'s 1 hour's work = (1/4 + 1/6) = 5/12

∴ A and B will fill the tank in 12/5hrs = 2 hrs 24 min.

So, II and III are needed.

∴ Correct answer is (B).

16. MATHEMATICAL REASONING

Answer Key

1. (B)	2. (D)	3. (C)	4. (B)	5. (B)	6. (A)	7. (C)	8. (C)	9. (C)	10. (C)
11. (A)	12. (C)	13. (D)	14. (B)	15. (C)	16. (B)	17. (B)	18. (D)	19. (A)	20. (C)
21. (A)	22. (B)	23. (B)	24. (B)	25. (A)					

1. **(B)**

Suppose Ravi gets x sums correct.

∴ Wrong sums = $2x$

Now $x + 2x = 96 \Rightarrow 3x = 96$.

$$\Rightarrow x = \frac{96}{3} = 32$$

2. **(D)**

From 1 to 100, there are ten numbers with 7 in unit's digit –

7, 17, 27, 37, 47, 57, 67, 77, 87,97. And ten number with 7 as ten's digit –

70, 71, 72, 73,74, 75, 76, 77, 78, 79.

Required number = 10 + 10 = 20

3. **(C)**

∴ 100 workers finish a work in 100 days

∴ 1 worker finish a work in 100 × 100

∴ 40 workers finish a work = $\dfrac{100 \times 100}{40}$

$\qquad\qquad\qquad\qquad = 250$ days

4. **(D)**

$$\frac{96}{x-4} - \frac{96}{x} = 4$$

$$\Rightarrow 96\left[\frac{1}{x-4} - \frac{1}{x}\right] = 4$$

$$\Rightarrow \frac{x-x+4}{x(x-4)} = \frac{4}{96}$$

$$\Rightarrow \frac{4}{x(x-4)} = \frac{1}{24}$$

$$\Rightarrow x^2 - 4x - 96 = 0$$

$$\Rightarrow x^2 - 12x + 8x - 96 = 0$$

$$\Rightarrow x(x-12) + 8(x-12) = 0$$

$$\Rightarrow (x+8)(x-12) = 0 \qquad (\because x \neq -8)$$

$$\Rightarrow x - 12 = 0 \Rightarrow x = 12$$

5. **(B)**

Let the number of women = x

Then number of men = $2x$

In city B,

$2x - 10 = x + 5$

$\Rightarrow 2x - x = 5 + 10$

$\Rightarrow x = 15$

Total number of passengers in the beginning

$= x + 2x = 3x = 3 \times 15 = 45$

6. **(A)**

D ↔ D ↔ D

I II III

Least no. of ducks = 3

7. **(C)**

Seven strike of clock = 6 intervals.

10 strikes have 9 intervals.

∴ 6 intervals have 7 sec and

∴ 1 interval have $\dfrac{7}{6}$ second

HINTS AND SOLUTIONS

$$\therefore \text{ 9 intervals have } \frac{7}{6} \times 9 = \frac{21}{2} = 10\frac{1}{2} \text{ sec.}$$

8. **(C)**

    Total ages of three people = 86 years
    Total ages of these three people after 2 years
    $$= 86 + 2 + 2 + 2$$
    $$= 92 \text{ years}$$

9. **(C)**

    Let the number of keepers be x.
    A/Q, Total number of feet
    $$= \text{total no. of heads} + 224$$
    $$\Rightarrow 50 \times 2 + 45 \times 4 + 8 \times 4 + 2 \times x$$
    $$= 50 + 45 + 8 + x + 224$$
    $$\Rightarrow 100 + 180 + 32 + 2x = 327 + x$$
    $$\Rightarrow 312 + 2x = 327 + x$$
    $$\Rightarrow 2x - x = 327 - 312$$
    $$\Rightarrow x = 15$$

10. **(C)**

    Number of students who did not pass
    $$= 450 - 270 = 180$$
    $$\therefore \text{ Percent} = \frac{180}{450} \times 100 = \frac{2}{5} \times 100 = 40\%$$

11. **(A)**

    Here, $x + 13x = 112$
    $$\Rightarrow 14x = 112 \Rightarrow x = \frac{112}{14} = 8$$

12. **(C)**

    Let d be the daughter and s be the son.
    $$d - 1 = s \Rightarrow d - s = 1 \quad \dots(1)$$
    $$2(s - 1) = d \Rightarrow 2s - d = 2 \quad \dots(2)$$
    From (1) and (2)
    $$-s + d = 1$$
    $$2s - d = 2$$
    $$\overline{}$$
    Adding $\quad s = 3$

13. **(D)**

    Total ages of 3 people = 96.
    Three years ago, total age of these 3 people
    $$= 96 - 3 - 3 - 3$$
    $$= 96 - 9 = 87 \text{ years}$$

14. **(B)**

    Let son's age be x.
    Mr. Sharma's age = $3x$.
    A/Q, $3x - 5 = 4(x - 5)$
    $$\Rightarrow 3x - 5 = 4x - 20$$
    $$\Rightarrow \qquad 4x - 3x = -5 + 20$$
    $$\Rightarrow \quad x = 15$$
    Age of Mr. Sharma = $3x = 3 \times 15 = 45$ years.

15. **(C)**

    Speed of train = 72 km/hr.
    $$= 72 \times \frac{5}{18} = 20 \text{m/sec.}$$
    $$\text{Time taken} = \frac{360}{20} = 18 \text{ seconds}$$

16. **(B)**

    Let x be the cost price.
    $$\Rightarrow x + 20\% \text{ of } x = 720$$
    $$\Rightarrow x + \frac{20x}{100} = 720$$
    $$\Rightarrow 120x = 100 \times 720$$
    $$\Rightarrow x = \frac{100 \times 720}{120} = 600$$

17. **(B)**

    Let Monu's age = x
    Manoj's age = $2x$
    A/Q, $2x - 3 = 3(x - 3)$
    $$\Rightarrow 2x - 3 = 3x - 9$$
    $$\Rightarrow 3x - 2x = 9 - 3$$
    $$\Rightarrow x = 6$$
    $$\Rightarrow \text{Present age of Manoj} = 2 \times 6 = 12 \text{ years.}$$

18. **(D)**

    The product of all the numbers in the dial of
    a telephone = 0

19. **(A)**

    Total number of handshakes
    $$= 9 + 8 + 7 + 6 + 5 + 4 + 3 + 2 + 1 = 45$$

20. **(C)**

    $$175 - 25 \div 5 + 20 \times 3 + 10$$
    $$= 175 \div 25 + 5 \times 20 - 3 \times 10$$
    $$= 7 + 5 \times 20 - 3 \times 10$$

$= 7 + 100 - 30$
$= 107 - 30 = 77$

21. (A)
$225 - 15 + 9 \times 15 \div 3$
$= 225 \div 15 \times 9 - 15 + 3$
$= 15 \times 9 - 15 + 3$
$= 135 - 15 + 3 = 123$

22. (B)
$23 \div 107 \times 135 - 5 + 3$
$= 23 + 107 - 135 \div 5 \times 3$
$= 23 + 107 - 27 \times 3$
$= 23 + 107 - 81$
$= 130 - 81 = 49$

23. (A)
$297 \times 57 \times 345 - 15 + 11 \div 18$
$= 297 - 57 - 345 \div 15 \times 11 + 18$
$= 297 - 57 - 23 \times 11 + 18$
$= 297 - 57 - 253 + 18$
$= 315 - 310 = 5$

24. (B)
$78 - 13 + 7 \times 6 \div 17 + 3$
$= 78 \div 13 \times 7 - 6 + 17 \times 3$
$= 6 \times 7 - 6 + 17 \times 3$
$= 42 - 6 + 51$
$= 93 - 6 = 87$

25. (A)
$123 \times 4 + 7 \div 76 - 19 + 7$
$= 123 - 4 \times 7 + 76 \div 19 \times 7$
$= 123 - 4 \times 7 + 4 \times 7$
$= 123 - 28 + 28$
$= 123$

<table>
<tr><td colspan="5" align="center">HOTS (ACHIEVERS SECTION)</td></tr>
<tr><td>26. (B)</td><td>27. (C)</td><td>28. (D)</td><td>29. (B)</td><td>30. (A)</td></tr>
</table>

26. (B)
Suppose Ravi gets x sums correct.
$\therefore$ Wrong sums $= 2x$
Now $x + 2x = 96 \Rightarrow 3x = 96.$
$\Rightarrow x = \dfrac{96}{3} = 32$

27. (C)
$\because$ 100 workers finish a work in 100 days
$\because$ 1 worker finish a work in 100×100
$\because$ 40 workers finish a work $= \dfrac{100 \times 100}{40}$

$\qquad = 250$ days

28. (D)
$\dfrac{96}{x-4} - \dfrac{96}{x} = 4$

$\Rightarrow 96 \left[\dfrac{1}{x-4} - \dfrac{1}{x} \right] = 4$

$\Rightarrow \dfrac{x - x + 4}{x(x-4)} = \dfrac{4}{96}$

$\Rightarrow \dfrac{4}{x(x-4)} = \dfrac{1}{24}$

$\Rightarrow x^2 - 4x - 96 = 0$
$\Rightarrow x^2 - 12x + 8x - 96 = 0$
$\Rightarrow x(x - 12) + 8(x - 12) = 0$
$\Rightarrow (x + 8)(x - 12) = 0 \qquad (\because x \neq -8)$
$\Rightarrow x - 12 = 0 \Rightarrow x = 12$

29. (B)
Let the number of women $= x$
Then number of men $= 2x$
In city B,
$2x - 10 = x + 5$
$\Rightarrow 2x - x = 5 + 10$
$\Rightarrow x = 15$
Total number of passengers in the beginning
$= x + 2x = 3x = 3 \times 15 = 45$

30. (A)
$D \leftrightarrow D \leftrightarrow D$
$\ \text{I} \qquad \text{II} \qquad \text{III}$
Least no. of ducks $= 3$

Answer Key

1. (C)	2. (A)	3. (B)	4. (A)	5. (D)	6. (C)	7. (A)	8. (C)	9. (C)	10. (D)
11. (D)	12. (A)	13. (A)	14. (A)	15. (C)	16. (C)	17. (A)	18. (D)	19. (D)	20. (A)
21. (C)	22. (C)	23. (A)	24. (C)	25. (C)	26. (A)	27. (C)	28. (A)	29. (B)	30. (A)

1. **(C)**
$7 \times 5 + 6 = 41$
$8 \times 7 + 5 = 61$
$6 \times 7 + 9 = 51$

2. **(A)**
$7 \times 4 + 3 \times 5 = 28 + 15 = 43$
$6 \times 2 + 6 \times 4 = 12 + 24 = 36$
$9 \times 3 + 5 \times 7 = 27 + 35 = 62$

3. **(B)**
$84 \div 7 + 42 \div 2 = 12 + 21 = 33$
$117 \div 13 + 96 \div 16 = 9 + 6 = 15$
$153 \div 17 + 63 \div 3 = 9 + 21 = 30$

4. **(A)**
This is a simple division series. Each number is divided by 5.

5. **(D)**
In this simple subtraction series, each number decreases by 0.4.

6. **(C)**
This is a simple multiplication series. Each number is 3 times more than the previous number.

7. **(A)**
The series is mopn/mopn/mopn/mopn. Thus, the pattern 'mopn' is repeated.

8. **(C)**
The series is bbccaa/ccaabb/aabbcc. Thus, the letter pairs move in a cyclic order.

9. **(C)**
The series is man/man/man/man/man. Thus, the pattern 'man' is repeated.

10. **(D)**
Each of the numbers is a prime number except 12.

11. **(D)**
Each of the numbers except 81 is a prime number.

12. **(A)**
In each number except 751, the difference of third and first digit is the middle one.

13. **(A)**
Each letter in the word is moved thirteen steps forward to obtain the corresponding letter of the code.

14. **(A)**
Each letter in the word is moved one step forward to obtain the corresponding letter of the code.

15. **(C)**
Each letter in the word is moved three steps forward to obtain the corresponding letter of the code.

16. **(C)**
Waiting, Wanting, Watching, Waving.

17. **(A)**
Lapse, Laurel, Leave, Leisure.

18. **(D)**
Project, Property, Protein, Proverb.

19. **(D)**
Because, wife of husband - herself; Brother of daughter - son. So, the man is Ritu's son.

20. **(A)**
Grandmother is one female, mother is another, wives of four sons are the four females and two daughters of all four sons are eight females. So, in all there are $1 + 1 + 4 + 8 = 14$ females.

21. **(C)**
Shalu is Mona's step-daughter, which means Shalu is the daughter of the other wife of Ravi. So, Shalu is the daughter of Leena or Leena is the mother of Shalu.

22. (C)

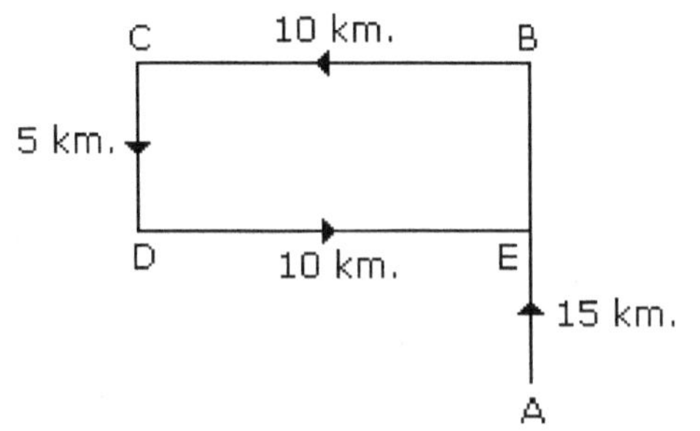

Therefore, it is clear that Lokesh is in the North from his house.

23. (A)

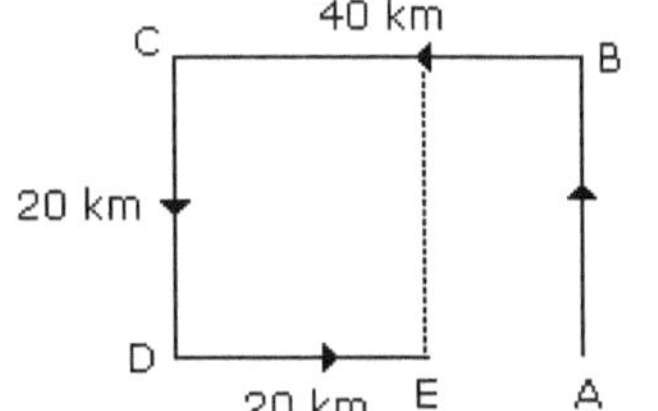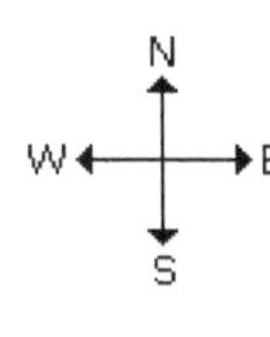

Required distance = BC − DE
$$= 40 - 20$$
$$= 20 \text{ km}$$

24. (C)

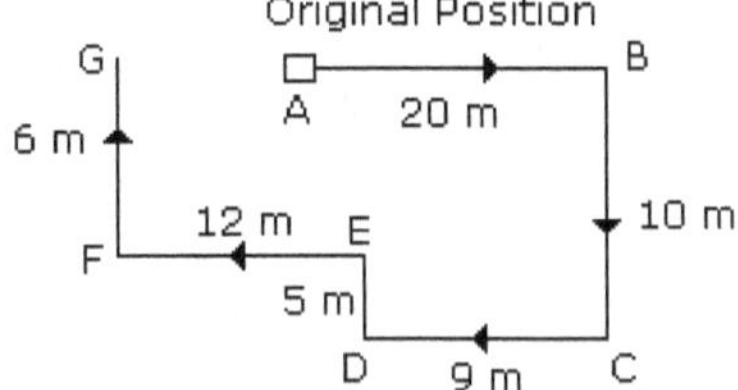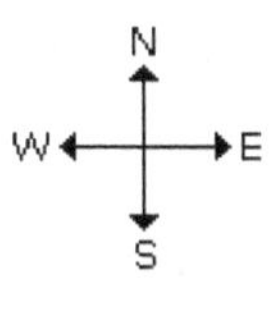

Therefore, it is clear that Sundar will face towards North.

25. (C)

5 7 8 9 7 6 5 3 4 2 6 8 9 7 5 2 4 6 2 9 7 6 4 7

8 9 7 6

26. (A)

2, 5, 8 all have frequency 3.

27. (C)

7 has highest frequency.

28. (A)

All other figures can be rotated into each other.

29. (B)

In each one of the figures except figure (2), three cups open towards the pentagon and two cups open outwards.

30. (A)

All other figures can be rotated into each other.

MODEL TEST PAPER

Answer Key

1. (A)	2. (A)	3. (B)	4. (C)	5. (B)	6. (B)	7. (D)	8. (A)	9. (C)	10. (A)
11. (C)	12. (C)	13. (B)	14. (A)	15. (B)	16. (D)	17. (C)	18. (C)	19. (B)	20. (B)
21. (A)	22. (A)	23. (B)	24. (C)	25. (B)	26. (C)	27. (A)	28. (C)	29. (A)	30. (C)
31. (D)	32. (D)	33. (B)	34. (C)	35. (C)	36. (C)	37. (C)	38. (B)	39. (A)	40. (A)
41. (D)	42. (B)	43. (D)	44. (B)	45. (A)	46. (D)	47. (A)	48. (D)	49. (B)	50. (B)

SAMPLE OMR ANSWER SHEET

1. STUDENT NAME (IN ENGLISH CAPITAL LETTERS ONLY)

Students must write and darken the respective circles completely using HB Pencil only. Othewise their Answer Sheets will not be evaluated.

PERSONAL DETAILS

2. SCHOOL CODE

3. CLASS

4. SECTION

5. ROLL NO.

6. QUESTION PAPER SET

A ◯
B ◯
C ◯
D ◯

7. MOBILE NUMBER

8. GENDER

MALE ◯
FEMALE ◯

9. STREAM
(Only for Class XI and XII Students)

MATHEMATICS ◯
BIOLOGY ◯
OTHERS ◯

MARK YOUR ANSWERS

	A	B	C	D		A	B	C	D
1.	Ⓐ	Ⓑ	Ⓒ	Ⓓ	26.	Ⓐ	Ⓑ	Ⓒ	Ⓓ
2.	Ⓐ	Ⓑ	Ⓒ	Ⓓ	27.	Ⓐ	Ⓑ	Ⓒ	Ⓓ
3.	Ⓐ	Ⓑ	Ⓒ	Ⓓ	28.	Ⓐ	Ⓑ	Ⓒ	Ⓓ
4.	Ⓐ	Ⓑ	Ⓒ	Ⓓ	29.	Ⓐ	Ⓑ	Ⓒ	Ⓓ
5.	Ⓐ	Ⓑ	Ⓒ	Ⓓ	30.	Ⓐ	Ⓑ	Ⓒ	Ⓓ
6.	Ⓐ	Ⓑ	Ⓒ	Ⓓ	31.	Ⓐ	Ⓑ	Ⓒ	Ⓓ
7.	Ⓐ	Ⓑ	Ⓒ	Ⓓ	32.	Ⓐ	Ⓑ	Ⓒ	Ⓓ
8.	Ⓐ	Ⓑ	Ⓒ	Ⓓ	33.	Ⓐ	Ⓑ	Ⓒ	Ⓓ
9.	Ⓐ	Ⓑ	Ⓒ	Ⓓ	34.	Ⓐ	Ⓑ	Ⓒ	Ⓓ
10.	Ⓐ	Ⓑ	Ⓒ	Ⓓ	35.	Ⓐ	Ⓑ	Ⓒ	Ⓓ
11.	Ⓐ	Ⓑ	Ⓒ	Ⓓ	36.	Ⓐ	Ⓑ	Ⓒ	Ⓓ
12.	Ⓐ	Ⓑ	Ⓒ	Ⓓ	37.	Ⓐ	Ⓑ	Ⓒ	Ⓓ
13.	Ⓐ	Ⓑ	Ⓒ	Ⓓ	38.	Ⓐ	Ⓑ	Ⓒ	Ⓓ
14.	Ⓐ	Ⓑ	Ⓒ	Ⓓ	39.	Ⓐ	Ⓑ	Ⓒ	Ⓓ
15.	Ⓐ	Ⓑ	Ⓒ	Ⓓ	40.	Ⓐ	Ⓑ	Ⓒ	Ⓓ
16.	Ⓐ	Ⓑ	Ⓒ	Ⓓ	41.	Ⓐ	Ⓑ	Ⓒ	Ⓓ
17.	Ⓐ	Ⓑ	Ⓒ	Ⓓ	42.	Ⓐ	Ⓑ	Ⓒ	Ⓓ
18.	Ⓐ	Ⓑ	Ⓒ	Ⓓ	43.	Ⓐ	Ⓑ	Ⓒ	Ⓓ
19.	Ⓐ	Ⓑ	Ⓒ	Ⓓ	44.	Ⓐ	Ⓑ	Ⓒ	Ⓓ
20.	Ⓐ	Ⓑ	Ⓒ	Ⓓ	45.	Ⓐ	Ⓑ	Ⓒ	Ⓓ
21.	Ⓐ	Ⓑ	Ⓒ	Ⓓ	46.	Ⓐ	Ⓑ	Ⓒ	Ⓓ
22.	Ⓐ	Ⓑ	Ⓒ	Ⓓ	47.	Ⓐ	Ⓑ	Ⓒ	Ⓓ
23.	Ⓐ	Ⓑ	Ⓒ	Ⓓ	48.	Ⓐ	Ⓑ	Ⓒ	Ⓓ
24.	Ⓐ	Ⓑ	Ⓒ	Ⓓ	49.	Ⓐ	Ⓑ	Ⓒ	Ⓓ
25.	Ⓐ	Ⓑ	Ⓒ	Ⓓ	50.	Ⓐ	Ⓑ	Ⓒ	Ⓓ

Signature of the Student & Date of Examination

Signature of the Invigilator & Date of Examination

V&S Publishers, F-2/16 Ansari Road, Daryaganj, New Delhi-110002, ☎ 011-23240026-27
✉ info@vspublishers.com, 🌐 www.vspublishers.com

www.ingramcontent.com/pod-product-compliance
Lightning Source LLC
LaVergne TN
LVHW060355200726
843506LV00003B/223